THE U~ ~~~

~

MANAGING THE PROBATION SERVICE

ISSUES FOR THE 1990s

Edited by Roger Statham and Philip Whitehead

LONGMAN

Published by Longman Industry and Public Service Management, Longman Group UK Limited, 6th Floor, Westgate House, The High, Harlow, Essex CM20 1YR, England and Associated Companies throughout the world.
Telephone: Harlow(0279) 442601
Fax: Harlow(0279) 444501
Telex: 81491 Padlog

A catalogue record for this book is available from The British Library

ISBN 0–582–09144–6

Typeset by Expo Holdings
Printed and bound in Great Britain

Dedication

This book is dedicated to
Wendy, Jonathan and Rachel;
and Frank and Elsie Whitehead

Contents

Biographical notes

Roger Statham

Roger Statham is Chief Probation Officer in Cleveland. He joined the Stoke service at the end of the 1960s and trained at Keele University. He has contributed to probation management training at regional and national levels and has published on management issues and cot death. He is happiest during the summer months when watching cricket.

Philip Whitehead

After completing his CQSW at Lancaster University in 1981, Philip Whitehead was appointed Probation Officer in Cleveland. In 1987 he became Research and Information Officer and later Information Manager. His publications include *Community Supervision for Offenders* (1990) and with two colleagues wrote *Probation, Temporary Release Schemes and Reconviction* (1991), both published by Avebury.

Bill McWilliams

Bill McWilliams has worked as Main Grade and Senior Officer. He spent four years in the Home Office Research Unit and ten years as Research Officer in the South Yorkshire service. Since 1984 he has been a Research Fellow at the Cambridge Institute of Criminology where he is Director of Studies of the Cropwood Programme and has published widely on probation and related topics.

Brian Fellowes

Brian Fellowes joined the probation service in 1967 and after fieldwork experience moved to Leeds Prison and became a Senior Probation Officer. He was appointed Probation Advisor, Prison

Service College in 1974 and in 1981 became Assistant Chief Probation Officer in Humberside. He has been involved in many aspects of training at area, regional, national and international levels and is currently working on secondment as Regional Training Coordinator in the North–East Region. He was elected a Senior Fellow of Hull University in 1991.

Roger Shaw

Roger Shaw is Chief Probation Officer of Powys and Research Fellow at the Cambridge Institute of Criminology. His probation experience was gained as a main grade and senior officer and as an Inspector of Probation. Before joining the criminal justice system in 1970 he worked in mining, industry and commerce in the UK and overseas including holding management positions. He has been involved in writing five books and a number of papers on aspects of criminal justice. His most recent book *Prisoners' Children: What are the Issues?*, was published in 1991 by Routledge.

Cedric Fullwood

Cedric Fullwood joined the probation service in 1963. He was appointed Director of Selcare Trust in 1977 and the following year moved to the Scottish Office as Deputy Chief Social Work Advisor. In 1982 he was appointed to his present job as Chief Probation Officer of the Greater Manchester service. He was chair of the Association of Chief Officers of Probation (ACOP) Finance and Resources Use Group in 1989 and, following a year as vice chair of ACOP, was elected chair in 1991.

Breidge Gadd

Breidge Gadd joined the probation service in 1969 and since that time has worked as a probation officer in both community and custodial settings. Her experience includes working with the Belfast Welfare Authority in 1969 and in the North–East of England during 1971. She has held a variety of managerial posts and was appointed Chief Probation Officer of the Northern Ireland service in 1986.

Mary Fielder

Mary Fielder started work as a probation officer in 1964 and eventually became Assistant Chief Probation Officer in 1979 with responsibility for the metropolitan districts of Wigan and Bolton. During 1983–1985 she was responsible for special developments, including the establishment of Day Centres following the 1982 Criminal Justice Act. From 1986–1991 she was Secretary to ACOPs Residential Services Committee and from 1988–1989 was seconded to work with the Audit Commission on a Value for Money Review of the probation service. In 1990 she was sponsored to visit the USA and Canada to examine the role of private and voluntary organisations in delivering services to offenders.

Lucia Saiger

Lucia Saiger started work for NACRO in 1984 at a day centre providing education for offenders. Between 1985–86 she completed an MA/CQSW course at Nottingham University before joining the Cleveland probation service. She became Senior Probation Officer in 1991. Her main interests are group work and the links between offending, drugs and alcohol.

Preface

Professor Ken Pease, Manchester

Every year for over a decade I taught probation students their criminology and had much other contact with them. Every year a new cohort of neophyte officers graduated whom one would meet occasionally thereafter. One of the most disturbing and consistent themes in their conversation was their frustration with probation management. Even when they had personal affection for the managers concerned, even when their own service was contrasted favourably with what they had heard of others, much more criticism than praise was expressed. The singers changed but the song did not. It continued for so long that the first cohorts of critics became the next generation of managers who also came in for criticism. The tensions are clearly something to do with service structure rather than with the good and decent people who work in it. A pastime of all organisations is bad-mouthing management, but there was an asperity in the comments of my former students which was, and is, worrying. I have also found probation managers over the same decade to have been very sensitive to external criticism, far more so than the police service over the same period. Some conflict in organisations is healthy, but at least to this writer many of the conflicts surrounding probation management do not feel good.

Into this context comes this book of readings, offering a variety of perspectives on the problems and challenges of probation management. Refreshingly free of a party line, each of the contributors to the book provides a distinct perspective on *how* to manage. A place is even found for Bill McWilliams's scepticism of the commonly understood role of managers (consultants still operate, professors still teach, so why shouldn't chief probation officers still advise, assist and befriend?). Interestingly, some of the most radical ideas come from the contributor closest in time to practice as a probation officer. Lucia Saiger was clearly impressed by the performance related payment (including dismissal for chronic performers) she found applied to probation officers in New York.

This links to a theme which I would have liked to see featuring more obviously in the book, and which I will use my privilege as preface writer to mention. The active ingredient in probation work is the probation officer. The counselling literature (and some criminological classics) tells us that some people influence the behaviour of others. Some people do not. Every year, as we launch another group of probation officers into an unappreciative world, I know which individuals I would back to change their clients. Sooner or later, service management will have to look objectively and systematically at which officers are diminishing the length or seriousness of the criminal careers of those with whom they are involved. How should managers manage that?

The solid achievements of this book are to present a catalogue of problems and many guides to good practice, but most of all to elicit an understanding of how difficult probation management is, and how many good ideas there are around. I will keep a few copies to lend to troubled new officers, or troubled new seniors. My usual criterion of a book's quality is whether it is ever returned from loan. I think I will run out of copies of this book quite quickly.

1   Introduction

Roger Statham and Philip Whitehead

The genesis of this book began in August 1990 with a casual conversation between the two editors. We happened to mention to each other that there was a paucity of literature about managerial issues in the probation service. The experience of one of us who was then working in middle and senior management training reinforced the need for ongoing debate about management in probation. Consequently the intention of this book is to focus attention on this debate and perhaps give it added impetus.

The contributors have been chosen to add to this debate and the issues touched upon below include: the origins of managerialism in the probation service; arguments for and against management; strategic thinking; empowerment; information systems; corporate management and managing intellectual resources; and the increasingly important subject of partnerships. Whilst we have attempted to include what we consider to be the most pertinent issues, we recognise it is not entirely comprehensive and any omission of what some readers consider to be important management issues is the responsibility of the editors. Having acknowledged our sins of omission, it is nevertheless hoped that the content of the book will provide an insight into some of the major management concerns around at the moment which are approached from different standpoints which reflect the rich and varied experiences and perceptions of the contributors themselves.

The chapters included are rooted in the probation service because one of our intentions is to demonstrate that there is a growing management ethic in the organisation. However, there has never been any intention to produce a book that would arrive at a management consensus because we recognise that the meaning of management itself could be debated endlessly. From the very outset our intention was to juxtapose a range of diverse views in the hope that differences of opinion and perspective would make a contribution to the management debate which is going on at the present time.

Despite the differences which emerge in the book all the chapters are linked together by the theme of change. The contributors would agree to this point if nothing else, which is that the probation service has gone through an unprecedented period of change during the last decade or so, and it seems that rapid change will continue for some time yet. Whilst there has been an attempt to put the book together in a cohesive and systematic way, it should be acknowledged that each chapter stands as a unique contribution in its own right. For the reader this presents the advantage of making the choice of reading the book from cover to cover and digesting it whole, or being more selective by using it as a reference book on key management subjects as the need arises.

We have no doubt that, in parts, the book will be seen as contentious. Some of the chapters explore tensions in the service and point the way forward against a background of shortcomings and deficiencies associated with the past. It may also at times seem over critical. However, we want the book to be seen as a statement of optimism in what can only be described as an uncertain future. It is also a statement of belief in the ability of the service to embrace a management culture which will ensure the organisation delivers a high quality service on behalf of customers to consumers, and makes an imaginative contribution to the work of the criminal justice system. The shape of things to come remains a matter of conjecture and speculation. However, we have tried in this book to shed some light on the way the service could and perhaps should evolve during the 1990s. Most of all we hope the book stimulates further debate on management issues in probation.

2 The rise and development of management thought in the English probation system

Bill McWilliams

Introduction

When the spy, George Blake, escaped from Wormwood Scrubs Prison on the evening of 22nd October 1966 he inadvertently set in train a series of events which proved to have profound effects on the probation service. Prior to that time, probation had largely been excluded from the managerial revolution which took root in the public and voluntary sectors from the late 1950s onwards but, in the wake of the escape, management thinking became established in the service and has since developed rapidly to the eminence seen today. In practical terms, Blake's escape played its part because it was followed immediately by an inquiry by Lord Mountbatten, conducted at high speed, and reporting in the same year. Lord Mountbatten's Report (Home Office, 1966a) was highly critical of security and made many recommendations but, relevant to the probation service, was the severe criticism of prison administration. The old–fashioned arrangements, the Report said, did not 'enable governors to use modern management techniques' (para. 21). This criticism was taken to heart by the Home Office and the development of management techniques speedily became a major focus in the prison service[1].

The year in which these events took place was also the year in which the probation service was given direct responsibility for all forms of aftercare and for prison welfare. Consequently, the service drew closer to the executive arm of the state, and many of the management insights and techniques being developed in prisons came to be shared by probation. Joint management training, seminars and conferences became the norm for the various supervisory grades in the two services. In comparison with the prison service, progress in the development of management was slow in the probation service, but a start had been made.

My purposes in this chapter are to trace the rise of management thought in the probation system, to explain the appeal which its doctrines hold for its many devotees, and to consider some of the substantial changes which its development has engendered. Additionally, because the introduction of managerial practices has met with a degree of resistance remarkable in an agency previously noted for placid industrial relations, I will consider the more important critiques of the management enterprise and explore the possibility of developing alternative means for the administration of the service.

Historical background

It would be possible to suggest that the first manager in the probation service was William Wheatley who, at the turn of the century, was running the probation services at the County of London Quarter Sessions (Home Office, 1910b)[2]. Following the implementation of the 1907 Probation of Offenders Act, Mr Wheatley had on his books some 500 probationers, supervised by fifteen assistants who reported to him. A typical line management arrangement it might be thought, but of course it was nothing of the kind. Mr Wheatley was a probation officer but, under the system of 'dual control' which operated at the time[3], he was also the head of the St Giles's Christian Mission which employed his assistants. Although responsible for his assistants, he clearly did not manage them in any modern sense. Rather, as he was closely involved with probationers himself, they were helpers who worked largely under their own initiative. The climate necessary to management to strike root was far in the future. Indeed, the Departmental Committee which reviewed the Probation Act after its first year of operation and interviewed Mr Wheatley, was firmly opposed even to the establishment of any hierarchy of authority in the service. As one of the Committee members said 'the danger, of course, of a chief probation officer is officialism and routine' (Home Office, 1910b, para. 789), and the Committee's Report emphasised the unfortunate consequences which would arise from placing probation officers in positions of subordination under chiefs (Home Office, 1910a, para. 50).

When the probation service was given responsibility for all forms of aftercare and for prison welfare its name was changed to the probation and aftercare service. The new name marked not only the new tasks assumed, but also a point of culmination in the rise of policy.

The rise of policy

The rise of modern ideas about policy in the probation service can be traced to the work and recommendations of two influential government committees[4]. The first of these was the Streatfeild Committee (Home Office and Lord Chancellor's Office, 1961), whose recommendations radically altered the pattern of social enquiry report provision in the criminal courts. For the first time a national policy was established to replace local customs, traditional arrangements and *ad hoc* interventions. Under the new policy it was no longer the individual offender who was considered for a social enquiry report, but rather classes of offenders defined by reference to the policy categories. The change, albeit apparently unnoticed at the time, was profound; henceforth individuals were to be seen as units in a policy formulation.

The second major influence upon the development of ideas of policy came hard on the heels of the first, it was the Report of the Advisory Council on the Treatment of Offenders (Home Office, 1963). In April 1961 the Home Secretary had asked the Advisory Council to review the arrangements for the organisation of statutory and voluntary aftercare for persons discharged from Borstals, prisons, detention centres and approved schools. The Council set up a subcommittee under the chairmanship of Mr J.B. Hartwell to carry out the review, and their report 'The Organisation of Aftercare', was published two years later.

The changes in the arrangements for aftercare which the Advisory Council proposed were sweeping. All the organisations which were then involved in aftercare (the Central After–Care Association, the National Association of Discharged Prisoners' Aid Societies, numerous local aid societies, and the Approved School Welfare Service) were to be wound down, and in their place the Council recommended:

- the amalgamation of compulsory and voluntary aftercare into a common service

- the employment of professional social workers on aftercare both in penal institutions and in the community, aftercare in the community, becoming the responsibility of an expanded and reorganised probation and aftercare service

- the decentralisation of the arrangements for aftercare, accompanied by a strengthening of the lines of communication between the social worker in the institution and colleagues in the community

- a greatly increased understanding of the part to be played by members of the community in the rehabilitation of offenders (Home Office, 1963, para. 215).

The practical arrangements which the Advisory Council proposed were based on the general policy of extending aftercare to as many offenders as possible. This was to be achieved partly by activating the provisions of the 1961 Criminal Justice Act which would bring substantially increased categories of offenders into the compulsory aftercare net, and partly by a considerable extension of voluntary aftercare. As with the recommendations of the Streatfield Committee, the policy identified classes of offenders to which aftercare would be applied rather than individual persons who might stand in need of it.

It is important to recognise at this point that the twin engine of policy development for the probation service which the Reports of the Streatfeild Committee and the Advisory Council created were not founded upon the modern preoccupation with reducing the prison population; rather the ultimate goal to which the policies of both the Committee and Council were directed was the scientific rehabilitation of offenders. As the Advisory Council said 'We conclude that the primary function of any system of aftercare must be the rehabilitation of the discharged offender' (Home Office, 1963, para. 22).

As we shall see in a moment, the proposals of the Streatfeild Committee and the Advisory Council had a profound effect on the organisation of the probation service. As these developments were taking place and the service was expanding rapidly and diversifying its tasks[5], there was a fundamental shift in the overarching goal of government policy away from the scientific rehabilitation of offenders towards the pragmatic imperative to relieve the pressure on the grossly overcrowded prison system. This led to a situation in which an organisational structure which was built to serve one purpose (rehabilitation) was pressed into another (the diversion of offenders from penal institutions). A crucial role which the Streatfeild Committee and the Advisory Council played in the moulding of the situation which pertains today is that they both, in their different ways, created the understanding that to be able to operate any policy it is necessary to have an administrative structure capable of doing so. Subsequently, that basic under-standing became elaborated into the insight that organisations and the persons within them require management if they are to function in the fulfilment of policy objectives. The structural basis chosen for the service, and that which would later give nurture to the managerial ethos, was bureaucracy. In one sense, given that the structure for the expanded service was being planned by civil servants the choice was inevitable, but it is important to note that the choice was not logically necessary; other forms of organisation could have been chosen.

The bureaucratisation of the English probation system

The history of the bureaucratisation of the English probation system has been documented, at least in broad outline by a number of writers (*see*, for example, Haxby, 1978; McWilliams, 1981) and we need not pursue too much detail here apart from noting some key historical events. The development of a hier-archical structure of authority within the probation service did not begin on any scale until the middle of the 1920s. As noted already, the first Departmental Committee on the service (Home Office, 1910a) was strongly opposed to the establishment of supervisory grades, but sixteen years later Rule 60 of the Probation Rules 1926, formally made it possible for the first time for probation committees, with the prior approval of the Secretary of State, to fix a special salary scale for principal probation officers who might be appointed to supervise the work of other probation officers[6]. Posts of senior probation officer followed and later still deputy and assistant principal, but areas were in no rush to make appointments and progress was slow. As late as 1962 when the Morison Committee reported (Home Office and Scottish Home Department, 1962), only sixty-two areas had appointed a prin-cipal officer and the remaining forty-one areas had not and, in the country as a whole, there were only 158 senior probation officers, an average of 1.5 per area. When Morison reported, however, the service was on the brink of immersion in its expanded duties in relation to aftercare and prison welfare. Once that plunge was taken in 1966 the process of bureaucratisation accelerated rapidly.

A key document in the history of the development of bureaucracy in the probation service was a circular issued by the Home
Office in 1966 (HOC 225/66) under the title 'Structure of the
Probation and Aftercare Service'. This circular was important in a
number of ways. First, it portrayed the principal probation officer
as being concerned solely with administration. This was a sharp
contrast to the findings of the Morison Committee which four
years earlier had envisaged principal officers directly supervising
offenders so as to be able to retain their professional skills and
keep in touch with local problems. Secondly, it introduced the
concept of line management. In aftercare work, the circular said,
the probation officer was no longer an officer of the court, but
rather worked to the probation committee through the principal
officer. Thirdly, because of the increased administrative burden,
principal probation officers needed extra help and this was to be
provided by a more extensive use of the senior grade and the
developed use of the assistant principal grade. Overall, the circular gave unprecedented encouragement to probation committees to make more senior and assistant principal appointments
and this despite there being a prices and incomes standstill in
force at the time.

Probation committees were quick to seize upon such
uninhibited encouragement. In the year in which the circular was
published the total number of probation officers was 2,557; ten
years later there had been an increase of over 100 percentage
points to 5,246. Unsurprisingly, in view of the encouragement
given, the proportion of supervisory grades more than kept pace
with the general growth, increasing from 14% of complement in
1961 to 22% in 1975 (Home Office, 1966b, 1979).

The development of a hierarchy of authority within the probation service was accompanied by an elaboration of rules, a
marked increase in specialisation, and a growth of impersonality.
By 1980, all the features of a classical Weberian bureaucracy were
in place. Of course, the structural changes did not go unremarked
and there were numerous complaints, some of which were
extremely bitter (*see*, for example, National Association of
Probation Officers, 1970; Colley, *et al.* 1970; and Allingham,
1975), but for many the process of bureaucratisation seemed
inevitable and quite beyond the power of any individual or group
to influence or halt. The authors of an influential report on the
management structure of the probation service (Joint Negotiating
Committee, 1980), for example, expressed their sympathy
towards officers suffering under the bureaucratic yoke, but
concluded nevertheless that they must be subject to 'managerial
oversight ... [to] ensure that the responsibilities of the service are

met at least to a minimum standard' (p.25). The managerial construct of the 'minimum standard' is one to which I shall return, but the Committee's conclusion was instructive in other ways also. It identified the complete change in focus which had taken place in probation from the individual officer who was the manifestation of the agency, to a service which contained and controlled the officer in pursuit of policy–directed objectives; objectives which under the new order belonged to the service rather than to the officer.

The advent and attraction of management thought

Newcomers to the probation service could be forgiven for assuming that management had always been an established part of the agency's life, but nothing could be further from the truth. Management, in any recognisable form, has been a presence in the probation service for about twenty years and with any degree of sophistication for only about ten years. As the phenomenon is so recent it will be useful to begin with a brief glance at what con-stituted the pre–managerial organisation. The best picture of that organisation is to be found in the Morison Report (Home Office and Scottish Home Department, 1962), which described the service as it functioned in the late 1950s and early 1960s. It is sometimes suggested by modern probation managers that before the importation of management thinking the service was, to put it crudely, something of a shambles. Further, these managers also suggest on occasion that the service could not now discharge its responsibilities or keep the Probation Rules without an overlay of managerialism[7]. This is entirely incorrect. In the Morison Report is described all the modern structure of the probation service; principal probation officers (re–designated 'chief' in 1974), deputy and assistant principals, and senior officers are all to be found, but there is no management, the concept simply does not appear. Rather, principal officers are depicted as the professional *administrators* of probation areas, supervising their subordinates but also, at least in some areas, carrying caseloads[8], and all senior probation officers, whilst providing supervision for officers, were also responsible for the direct oversight of offenders. As I have noted, this was seen as important for all grades in retaining skills and keeping in touch; it was surely also crucial in retaining a *professional* identity. In a profession the most senior members, no matter how eminent, practise their professional skills; the consultant surgeon operates on patients, the university professor teaches students, the greatest lawyer appears in court, and so on. A principal, or chief, probation officer in order to be a probation officer needs to be in personal touch with the supervision of offenders. The fact that this proposition may seem strange, even eccentric, in today's probation service merely serves to measure the distance which the service has travelled along the managerialist road and to underline the extent to which a professional identity has been lost.

The probation service of the early 1960s, as portrayed by Morison, was based on a professional–administrative model of organisation. It must be reiterated that despite its lack of managerialism it was a model which worked. Under it, the professional skills of probation officers were seen as being enhanced by enabling administrative provision, and the quality of their work ensured by a specific type of supervision. It would probably be agreed generally that some parts of that model persist to the present day; equally however, much of the model has been supplanted by the steady development of managerial control over the professional conduct of probation officers and the retreat of the higher grades from the professional task.

The rise of management

The introduction and consolidation of management control over professional activity represented a major shift in the nature of the organisation and in its understanding of itself. The self- motivating probation officer, bound by rules of conduct and answerable mainly to the courts was gradually replaced by the managerially controlled officer bound by a hierarchy of authority and answerable, through that hierarchy, to the executive. In practical terms, this profound change rested crucially on one key concept which was drawn from the old, professional–administrative service and injected into the new, managerial service in transmuted form; that concept was supervision. The change in meaning which the term 'supervision' underwent was captured in the Butterworth Report (Department of Employment, 1972). Butterworth remarked that in the probation service the notion of supervision was closer 'to the academic use of the word than to industry's understanding of it, that is to say, it is normally a consultation between supervisor and supervised with the main grade officer being questioned in the course of discussions or conferences about casework' (para.107). And of 'management' the Report said that this was seen in the service 'largely as an extension of supervision [and] as an enabling function providing facilities for the main grade officers to perform their work satisfactorily' (para.108). But the Report acknowledged that a new situation was coming into being and it linked this with the larger range of activities, saying that increasingly 'management is required to perform a planning and controlling function, as the service takes on responsibilities for new activities such as probation or bail hostels and aftercare work involving the use of volunteers' (para. 108).

Although one of the details was not correct, [9]there seems little to quarrel with in Butterworth's assessment; growth, and the diversification of activities were seen as requiring new ideas about management and new, controlling managerial functions. Thus it was that the 'supervision' by principal and senior officers which in the old probation service the Morison Report defined as 'modern ... casework supervision' (p.155) became, in the new service, a function of control in pursuit of policy objectives. The Management Structure Review (Joint Negotiating Committee, 1980) summed up the change as follows:

> It is no longer sufficient to look upon management ... as purely a means of enabling probation officers to practice their social work skills. Whilst management is still concerned with the provision of an appropriate work setting ... it is seen as having to do far more than this. Its primary task is to identify the tasks which society requires of the service, and to develop ways of discharging those responsibilities most effectively (p.9).

And the first of the 'functions of management' which the Review went on to identify was to formulate policy and set objectives. There is, of course, a certain irony in this. In the heady days of the late 1970s and early 1980s the progress of management seemed inexorable and managers were coming to think that they embodied the spirit of the probation service *in propria persona*. They sincerely believed that as managers they formulated policy and held the fate of a distinguished public service in their hands. The realisation that this is not the case has dawned slowly but nonetheless painfully; although it is still denied by some[10], the more astute among the management ranks have come to recognise that the formulation of policy takes place in government departments and that managers are but the technicians of the policy will. Of course, as one chief probation officer remarked to me recently, there is still some room for managers to negotiate with policy makers over detail, but that is small recompense for the near- transformation which has taken place in the service over recent years from a probation agency towards a correctional agency. This is not a movement which many have desired and was not foreseen when chief officers first set foot on the management road.

The attraction of management thought

As I have noted already, the profound changes which were wrought in the probation service through the acquisition of aftercare, bureaucratisation, and the development of policy had as their overarching goal the rehabilitation of offenders[11]. Yet at the very time that the organisational machine was being developed to pursue this goal, doubts about the efficacy of penal treatments were growing and belief in them was officially abandoned in the 1970s. The government's Review of Criminal Justice Policy 1976 (Home Office, 1977) concluded starkly that 'little can be done to "cure" criminals, and that no one type of sentencing measures applied generally is more likely to achieve reform than any other' (p.48). The magnitude of the blow which this represented to probation officers cannot be overestimated; as one chief probation officer put it, the painful conclusion had to be that 'the certainties of our knowledge–base had gone' (Thomas, 1978). The profound nature of the shock which this caused has probably not been fully appreciated; its effects were far–reaching and touched each practitioner personally. One consequence of this body blow to the treatment ethic was an urgent struggling towards a new ideal which might replace it. For some in the service an ideal was to be found in Marxist analysis and an attempt to develop socialist practice (*see*, Walker and Beaumont, 1981); for others the quest was for a reconceptualisation of treatment and the development of personalist approaches (*see*, Bottoms and McWilliams, 1979); but the ideal which attained dominance was that of management. This was not a dominance, it should be said, which sprang from universal acclaim, but rather was achieved by imposition and accepted with reluctance. The rhetoric of 'a well–managed agency, was difficult for modern politicians to resist no matter what the actuality on the ground, and support was forthcoming from many of those in positions of authority in the service; ultimately, for them, the strength of the desire for a restoration of certainty was sufficiently overwhelming to quell the doubts. Of course, this did not apply to all of those who were to become the managers of the new service; one widely-respected chief officer of a large proba-tion area, Bill Weston (1973) had this to say:

> As the term 'management' comes into social work from the field of industry, so does the old notion of essential

competition, in which the managers and workers are both seen as being in opposition to each other ... [In] the probation and aftercare service, the objectives of the main grade officer and those of the chief officer are essentially the same, a concept which, if grasped and its possibilities maximised, can lead to more mature relationships ... than when cruder management/worker concepts are allowed to prevail (p.70).

Weston's analysis proved to be prescient, but his optimism, unhappily, was misplaced. The concept of shared objectives has not prevailed and indeed, because of the mismatch between professional and managerial goals, it could not be expected to do so. To understand why that is so we need to consider a critique of management.

A critique of management

It is sometimes held that whilst management is a possibility at the level of modal ontology, it does not actually exist. More plausible is the argument that although management exists it does not operate on the bases of the current models of rational managerial action. Particularly suspect are the supposedly high–powered information processing and decision analysing aspects of the managerial function. Empirical evidence from the United States suggests that these are myths[12]. As I have suggested, a chief probation officer who embraces the management ideal becomes a technician of the policy will, and a useful shorthand is to see the manager as representing 'policy in action'. Nevertheless, it would be a mistake to see management as simply sets of techniques, certain in their value–neutrality and even–handedness; it is much more. The management ideal is based on a system of thought which embraces, amongst other things, ideas on the status of knowledge, the nature of persons, and the ethics of action. Thus, any satisfying analysis of management must include attention not only to its putative objective–related efficiency, but also to its theoretical bases.

Management does not exist in a vacuum, and in attempting to assess the worth of its ideal in the probation service it is necessary to identify some object which can act as a touchstone; such an object is not hard to find. There is in the service a system of ideas about the practice of supervising offenders which has evolved over a lengthy period of time, pre–dating the management ethic by many years. This is the ideal of probation practice. This ideal, despite recent changes, forms a central part of the culture of the agency and goes a long way towards identifying the nature of the professional tradition of being a probation officer. In what follows, I will elaborate on this ideal and then contrast it with managerial thought.

The ideal of probation practice

In recent times the probation ideal has suffered such an overlay of bureaucratic thought and action that it is difficult to stand back and remember that its essence is profoundly simple. The web of policy, procedures and performance indicators woven around it has obscured the central meaning of the probation system, and it is necessary to remind ourselves precisely what it is. One of the finest statements of the ideal, and one of the earliest, was made by Archbishop William Temple when he gave the foundation Clarke Hall Fellowship lecture in 1934. He said that in administering punishment the community has three interests to consider: the maintenance of its own life and order; the interests of individual members generally; and the interests of the offender. He thought that this was the necessary order of priority, but that it would be wrong to leave any of the interests out. Particularly, he said that if the interest of the offender was omitted the action would lose its quality of punishment and deteriorate into vengeance. This is because the offender would then no longer be treated within the society taking penal action, but against it, and therefore outside it. The Archbishop provided a way of understanding offenders which lies at the heart of a probation officer's work. We are not what we appear, he said 'but what we are becoming; and if that is what we truly are, no penal system is fully just which treats us as anything else' (p.39). He concluded that:

> though retribution is the most fundamental element in penal action, and deterrence for practical reasons the most indispensable, yet the reformative element is not only the most valuable in the sympathy which it exhibits and in the effects which it produces, but it is also that which alone confers upon the other two the full quality of justice. It is here that the whole system of probation fits into the scheme ...; the work of probation officers... should not be regarded as a dispensable though estimable adjunct to the administration of justice, but as an essential part of it without which it cannot be altogether just (p.40).

The probation ideal, therefore, is quite simple that offenders should reform and turn away from crime. This is entirely in accord with government policy and hence might be seen as unproblematic. The simplicity of the ideal is beguiling, however, and it is necessary to make a distinction between the ideal itself and the ideal of probation practice. By the latter I mean that system of beliefs, understandings and precepts for professional action which probation officers have painstakingly built over many years of thought and experience. I cannot emphasise too strongly that the ideal of practice is not a static object, immutable at a given point of time. Rather it is constantly evolving and developing, and indeed one of the principal strengths of the model of organisation which I shall put forward later is that the process of evolution and development is enhanced by being made more formal than at present and raised in level by rationality and sensibility in choice. The probation ideal has always stood at the mercy of those determined to see reform as a matter for coercion, and this has been most clearly manifest in the confusion which has surrounded the enforcements of the requirements of orders and licences and the desire that offenders should be reformed. The nub of the matter is that whilst officers have a clear duty to enforce requirements, that enforcement cannot properly be extended to reformation, and this is where the ideal of probation practice collides headlong with those who see coercive reform as an acceptable extension of penal action. From the very beginning of the probation system the pressures towards coercive reformation have been powerfully manifest. Some of those pressures have arisen externally, but others have come from within the service itself. For example, Ayscough (1923) reports on one of the first missionary officers who complained in 1877 that he had 'some fearful cases to deal with', was 'baffled to know what to do with them' (p.23), and emerged with a coercive solution: and many years later the Principal Probation Officers' Conference (1968) concluded that practice must 'lean heavily on a degree of coercion' (p.7).

In more recent times probation officers have been increasingly wary of the coercive approach to reform. The moral ground for rejecting it is a strong one: persons should be treated at all times as ends in themselves rather than as means to an end. There is also the practical ground that coercive reformation does not work. Most probation officers know that offenders cannot be bullied into reform and that the temptation to try must be resisted. If that position is accepted, and many probation officers do accept it, we can see at once that it fits badly with the present, policy–driven precepts of management. The current emphasis in policy on toughness, punishment and confrontation in the supervisory process seems set to upset the delicate balance which probation officers have been able to achieve in their dealings with offenders.

Of course, the requirements of orders and licences should be enforced rigorously, such is a probation officer's duty; but confrontation and bullying are quite different matters and are certainly at variance with the ideal of probation practice.

Another area in which managerial and practice thought seem set to clash is that of the procedure code. Recent years have seen the introduction of procedural codes and practice handbooks drawn up by managers[13], and currently national standards are being introduced in respect of a number of areas of work. It has to be said, however, that such measures are not unproblematic. In some circumstances, standardisation is desirable, but not invariably so; the idea that bureaucratic even–handedness is an unconditional good is mistaken; even–handedness does not always equal fairness, much depends on the circumstances of the recipients concerned. Procedure codes and the like have three main disadvantages: they legislate only for a minimum standard; they relocate discretion up a hierarchy away from the professional practitioner; and they shift attention away from individual persons. It must be emphasised that to accord with the ideal, probation practice in relation to reform is necessarily highly individual. It rejects coercion and, because it is about liberating persons and confirming their autonomy in order that they may make genuinely free choices, it also rejects manipulation. In an age much preoccupied with technique, function and utilitarian ends it is continuously necessary to reiterate the worth of the probation ideal and the values upon which it rests. There is a clash between this ideal and the instrumentalism of the techno-cratic consciousness of management, but technical knowledge can be balanced and held in check by what Michael Whan (1986) has called 'moral knowledge'. With moral knowledge one 'cannot know in advance, as with technical knowledge, what constitutes the proper means to some end, nor what is good' (p.247). Moral knowledge, he says, requires 'not only self–understanding, but also the understanding that reaches beyond oneself to another person (p.249). It is only in this way, he argues, that one can

> begin to try to determine what is good in a particular situation
> ... In understanding another's experience and actions, one
> must have an idea of the other's sense of rectitude. One must
> be able to comprehend ... the purposes which the other has in
> doing something. This shared understanding takes the form of
> a dialogue ... One cannot fully understand without hearing the
> other's reasons and grounds. In giving this hearing, one
> expresses a tacit respect for what the other has to say, even if
> one then disagrees with it (p.249).

A major contribution to understanding in this area, highly relevant to the ideal of probation practice, has been made by the moral philosopher, Alasdair MacIntyre. Writing on practice, MacIntyre (1981) holds that the goods which are to be had from, and are internal to, a practice based on moral knowledge are not instrumental goods. Rather they are the expressive goods that 'human powers to achieve excellence, and human conceptions of the ends and goods involved, are systematically extended' (p.175). These goods are realised in the course of trying to achieve the standards of excellence which are appropriate to the practice and partly define it. For MacIntyre, excellence in practice is to be had only through the exercise of the virtues of justice, courage and honesty. The implication of this for the supervision of offenders by probation officers is that practice should be contained within and given a direction by these virtues. All persons who stand in a professional relationship with probation officers must be treated with equity; good practice requires the courage to take risks where appropriate; and truthfulness is vital for the denial of manipulation. There is a potential for lack of accord with the management ethic here. If these writers are correct, then managerial procedure codes simply cannot specify, *a priori*, precisely how these virtues are to be expressed in particular instances in the myriad social interactions which constitute practice. As Michael Whan has convincingly argued, what constitutes the good in a given situation is specific to that situation, and thus achievement in the art of being a probation officer is reaching an excellence in practice which is situation–specific[14].

The foregoing sketch of the ideal of probation practice is far from complete, but perhaps it will give a sufficient indication of the issues to stand as a counterpoise to the management ideal to which we must now turn. In what follows I touch first on management as a model for the arrangement and conduct of organisations, and then consider some of its most common theoretical claims.

The management model of organisations

Management as a conceptual framework has become so deeply embedded in our culture that the ways in which management is supposed to operate within organisations, and the nature of the managerial enterprise are often taken as being obvious. Nevertheless, the term 'management model' is often applied loosely to a varied range of organisational arrangements and social interactions. Consequently, it will be as well to begin with a brief characterisation of what I intend to mean in this chapter when I speak of the 'management model of organisation'. The essential elements of the model were stated early in the century by Frederick Taylor (1911). Management, he said, 'is knowing exactly what you want men to do and then seeing that they do it in the best and cheapest way possible' (p.23). These basics have been much elaborated over time, but they remain of the essence. Consider how the oft–quoted Management Structure Review (Joint Negotiating Committee, 1980) applied them to the probation service. It said that the task of management was to 'set objectives; to organise the undertaking ... and activities necessary to achieve the objectives; to classify the work so that it may be ... assigned to individuals and groups; to provide supervision, support and training; [and] to measure actual performance against the original plan' (p.9). The elements of the management model are set out in Figure 1.1.

We should note that the model is linear. It begins with a given policy, proceeds through the translation of policy into instrumental objectives and the specification of practice held to be commensurate with the objectives; and ends with practice monitoring and the correction of any practice found to be non–commensurate with the objectives. It may be that the model is appropriate in the industrial settings from whence it was derived, but in a professional agency it has marked disadvantages:

- the chances of modifying incorrect policies are low

- discretion is relocated from professionals to managers

- professional innovation and risk-taking are curtailed

Given Policy

↓

Managers translate policy into
instrumental objectives

↓

Specification by managers of
objective–commensurate practice

↓

Managerial practice–monitoring to
confirm commensurability with objectives or to correct
non–commensuration

Figure 1.1   The management model

- the quality of practice can be guaranteed only to a minimum standard
- chief probation officers are transmuted into managers
- the probation service becomes vulnerable to imposed changes in its nature.

The last of these disadvantages is the most important. A probation service operating under the management model is susceptible to changes in its nature at the will of policy makers. Thus, it could be transformed into a community correctional agency, for example (a direction in which the English probation service is heading rapidly), or it could be changed into an agency of general community punishment. Perhaps in today's punitive climate society desires agencies of that kind, but I suspect that were it to be effectively abolished by such changes, the probation service would leave a vacuum which would eventually come to be filled; filled perhaps by the sort of voluntary effort in which the service had its roots. Certainly, if we accept Archbishop Temple's analysis, the penal system would be the poorer for the loss of the service; but these are not matters which can be addressed here; rather we must now consider the management ideal.

The management ideal

The manager is such a taken–for–granted figure in modern life that an evaluation of the management ideal poses the problem of how the managerial enterprise is to be judged. Three claims appear to be central to the management ethic; that it is of universal applicability to organisations; that it is effective; and that its effectiveness in goal achievement is morally neutral. I will consider these seriatim.

In relation to universal applicability, we may note first that whilst management techniques may be applied to many organisations, it is not necessary for their proper conduct. As I have noted, the probation service managed for the greater part of its history without management, and many organisations discharge their functions perfectly well without recourse to management. But advocates of management sometimes support the claim to universal applicability by the assertion that managers in one field can easily translate their skills into another. It may be suggested, for example, that the manager of a business who is effective in maximising profit could be equally effective in managing a probation service, but the falsity of applying the conceptual framework of trade to professional relationships was identified recently by Daragh Lawless (1989). In trade transactions, he points out, the concern is with a product; in a professional transaction the concern is with a person. A tradeable product and the outcome of a professional encounter are totally different. The first is objective and reproducible, the second is specific to the person concerned and thus unique. In contrast to a commercial product, the outcome of a professional transaction can never be mass–produced, nor can it be determined in advance by management edict or transferred between recipients.

The claim to effectiveness is central to the management ideal, but this too is of dubious applicability to probation. Effectiveness is not a fixed and immutable object which can be used as a steadfast measure of the worth of action; rather it varies over time and between circumstances. A glance at the history of the probation system demonstrates this. In the age of the missionary probation officer the ultimate objective of action was to hasten the establishment of God's kingdom on earth through the saving of offenders' souls. To be effective then, as one missionary officer explained (Potter, 1927), probation work had to be 'a piece of Christ–like effort ... whose object is the same as His, to seek and to save that which was lost' (p.ix). With the rise of putatively scientific understandings of offenders and their treatment, the notion of effectiveness changed. The new insight was that effective probation could cure offenders of the psycho–social illness of their offending. Now, however, that objective has been abandoned and the development of policy to control offending as an aggregate phenomenon of social activity has replaced concern with individual offenders. Today, effectiveness is related to the success of imposed social control[15]. When effectiveness is such a variable concept, it cannot properly be used to justify the management enterprise in probation.

The claim which management makes to moral neutrality is also open to question. As Alasdair MacIntyre (1981) points out, effectiveness is not morally neutral and 'the whole concept of effectiveness is inseparable from a mode of human existence in which the contrivance of means is in central part the manipulation of human beings into compliant patterns of behaviour; and it is by appeal to his own effectiveness in this respect that the manager claims authority within the manipulative mode' (p.71).

On this analysis, therefore, the claims of management to universal applicability, effectiveness and moral neutrality are open to grave doubt. MacIntyre concludes that management represents 'the obliteration of the distinction between manipulative and non–manipulative social relations' (p.29). If that is a correct conclusion, then it is clear that the management model fits badly with the ideal of probation practice. Probation practice, if it is to aspire to excellence, must eschew manipulation. For practitioners to strive towards that excellence within an organisational model based on the very manipulation which the ideal repudiates severely handicaps them.

Because the management ethic has penetrated so deeply into every aspect of agency life, I must accept that the views expressed above are unlikely to win the acclaim of managers in the probation service. Not only that, the management ideal is now pursued across a wide range of public agencies, and probation is but one of many professional groups to fall under management control. Nevertheless, it may rightly be said that the critic of the spread of bureau–managerialism need never feel lonely. As management has grown so has the number of its critics, and the scope and persistence of their criticisms across a whole range of professional occupational groups suggests that it would not be entirely inappropriate to consider if a viable alternative might be developed. Such an alternative would need to take account of the criticisms, would need to give support to the probation ideal, but would also need to be able to demonstrate how the issues of accountability and standards of service would be tackled. Not without trepidation, I set out such an alternative below in the hope that it will be taken as an invitation to discussion and criticism.

A professional–administrative model of organisation

Christopher Hodgkinson (1983), in his book on the philosophy of leadership, takes the view that in modern times ontology, which deals with the nature of being or reality, plays but little part in the life of organisations today (p.4). He is undoubtedly correct, and the starting point for my proposed professional–administrative model of organisation is the need to reinstate and give prominence to ontological concerns. I take the view, for example, that it is of the utmost importance to know what a probation officer *is* as a prerequisite to knowing what she or he does. Similarly, I think it is of great moment to know what the probation service *is*, and what a chief probation officer *is*. Consequently, the professional–administrative model which I suggest as a substitute for management begins with reflection on the nature of the probation service. The model as a whole is shown in Figure 1.2.

The understandings to which the reflection on the nature of the probation service give rise assist in the second stage of the

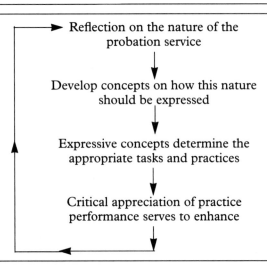

Figure 1.2   A professional–administrative model

process, the development of ideas about how the nature of the agency should be expressed. In turn, the expressive concepts so derived determine what the appropriate tasks for the service are, and they are also prescriptive of the sorts of practices which are congruent with the initial ontological understandings. Thus the model flows from ontology to practice. All practice is then subject to critical appreciation and the fresh awareness which this produces is fed back to the beginning of the process and aids in the reflections on the nature of the agency. Unlike the management model, therefore, which is linear, this model is circular. Circularity is sometimes equated with a lack of progress, but I should emphasise that this is not the case here. What is taken back in the circle are the constantly fresh insights derived from the evolving world of practice and enhanced by critical appreciation. In MacIntyre's terms, what is taken back are the conceptions of the ends and goods involved in practice.

As will be apparent, the central emphasis in this model is on professional practice. This is because ultimately what really counts in service organisations are the events which occur at the point of delivery of the service to which the agency is devoted. The finest policies, the highest technology, the most elaborate procedural codes, and the most definitive hierarchies of authority count for nothing if the professional action at the point of service is defective. That said, it is also of great importance to have efficient administration, and in this model the administration rests on clear leadership within the critical culture which is of the model's essence[16]. Leadership is desirable in the exercise of practice. As

MacIntyre (1981) says, when one enters a practice, one joins:

> a relationship not only with its contemporary practitioners, but
> also with those who have preceded us in the practice,
> particularly those whose achievements extended the reach of
> the practice to its present point. It is thus the achievement,
> and *a fortiori* the authority, of a tradition ... from which I have
> to learn. And for this learning and the relationships to the past
> which it embodies the virtues of justice, courage and
> truthfulness are prerequisite (p.181).

Thus, whilst a manager is but 'policy in action', a leader
represents 'philosophy in action' and embodies the authority of
achievement within the tradition of a practice. Despite this clear
distinction, it is sometimes held that management can give leadership in the service, but that is not the case. Achievement in
management is measured against the extent it is effective in the
manipulative mode, and manipulation and leadership are incom-
patible. A moment's reflection assures us that persons who are led
towards some intrinsic good are free to bring, in their striving for
that good, their own personal and unique powers. Persons who
are manipulated as means towards the realisation of another's end
are restricted in the exercise of their personal powers. Thus, the
practice which they represent, is not enhanced in this manipulative mode; rather it becomes atrophied and ultimately the tradition withers and dies for want of fresh thought and development.

The concept of administration which this model employs is
very different from that of management. Christopher Hodgkinson
(1978) makes the distinction which applies. He says:

> We mean by *administration* those aspects dealing more with
> the formulation of purpose, the value–laden issues, and the
> human component of organisations. By *management* we mean
> those aspects which are more routine, definitive,
> programmatic, and susceptible to quantitative methods ...
> Administration is ends–oriented, management is
> means–oriented. The pure administrator is a philosopher, the
> pure manager is a technologist (p.5).

In the professional–administrative model, the role of the chief
probation officer is of key importance. S/he embodies, *in propria
persona*, the professional practice tradition, and it also stands at
the head of the administration of the service. Such a model is to
be found in our universities where the vice chancellor heads the
administration and simultaneously embodies the academic ideal.

Finally, it is necessary to say something about accountability
under the proposed model. The need for public services to be

accountable is sometimes held to be the reason that they need management, but the argument is not valid and seems to arise from the conflation of the concept of accountability with two other ideas. The first idea is that of a hierarchy of authority; it is held that actions can be properly accounted for only through a line of authority, but that is not so. Individual professional practitioners can be called to account for their actions and are capable of giving such an account directly without an overlay of line management. The second idea confused with accountability is that of a strict adherence to policy directives. For example, it was suggested to me recently by a senior Home Office official that my professional–administrative model could not work because it might lead to lack of accountability by generating action at variance with policy. It is true that the model might engender a questioning of some aspects of policy, but this has nothing to do with accountability. Accountability, as the word implies, means being able to give an account of the reasons for action. Such an account and the actions described may then be judged according to their rightness. In a sense, accountability can on occasions be the very opposite of adherence to policy. Where policy is wrong, an account of action which merely said, in effect, 'I obeyed orders' is not in the public interest and is simply not good enough for a rational moral agent.

We may see accountability proper as being of two kinds: formal accountability, and substantive accountability. Formal accountability is associated with the management model and its object is to show that if errors occur the organisation is not at fault, or only minimally so. Accountability in this sense involves pointing to the correct procedures which exist to minimise the risk of errors and by demonstrating that these procedures are regularly espoused and checked by the responsible managers. The main response to unfortunate incidents is the elaboration of procedures and checks to try to ensure that the event does not recur. The main problems with formal accountability are that it inhibits desirable risk–taking, and it tends to diminish personal responsibility. Substantive accountability, which is associated with the professional–administrative model, in contrast, has the object of so arranging matters that if error occurs it is possible for individual persons to take the lessons into their hearts and into their practices. This is achieved not by an elaboration of procedural codes, since such codes can never cover all contingencies, but rather by trying to identify any general practice principle which might have been violated in a given incident, and thus to create fresh understandings of the principle and its place in the generality of good practice.

Conclusions

A senior politician enquired recently if the probation service 'had been around for a while?' I suspect that this level of awareness is fairly common among policy makers and, although it is alarming, it is also useful in alerting us to the need to iterate and reiterate the essential simplicity of the idea of probation and its history in penal thought. As with most worthwhile social institutions, the essence of probation, based in notions of mercy and an opportunity to reform, is not complicated. Its nature has been adversely altered in the 1991 Criminal Justice Act by its translation into a sentence, but the central idea remains and retains its validity.

Over the years the simple core of probation has been overlaid by successive forms of complexity. Initially, the overlay was of religious fervour and its attendant self–righteousness and intolerance. This was followed by an overlay of 'scientific' treatment and its accompanying coercive reformation; and today the overlay is of management with its concomitant manipulation. The coverings to simplicity have always taken a misplaced form. David Garland (1990) has suggested recently that penal institutions

> should be seen – and should see themselves – as institutions for the expression of social values, sensibility, and morality, rather than an instrumental means to a penological end ... the pursuit of values such as justice, tolerance, decency, humanity, and civility should be part of any penal institution's self–consciousness–an intrinsic and constitutive aspect of its role–rather than a diversion from its 'real' goals or an inhibition of its capacity to be 'effective' (pp. 291–2).

Surely these precepts apply with great force to the probation service and here is a real reason for importing a complexity which might be acceptable. If the institution of probation were to follow Garland's precept and attempt to become an expression of social values and morality, then although the fundamental idea would retain its simplicity, the practice would need to be complex and subtle indeed. Thus, I argue in probation simplicity should yield to complexity and subtlety when we move into the arena of a practice concerned with the virtues. This practice of care and concern for offenders stands at the pinnacle of the agency's achievement and it requires rigorous intellectual effort to approach its ideal whilst avoiding the pitfalls of romanticism and sentimentality. Given the nature of this book, we must ask what part the management ethic might have to play in this fresh effort?

The answer must be, very little. No matter how generously con-
strued, management remains instrumental and manipulative and
such qualities have little to bring to a practice ideal which is at
one expressive and liberating.

Notes

1. A comparison of the Reports of the Work of the Prison Department for the
    years 1963 (Home Offices 1964) (pre-Mountbatten) and 1967 (Home Office
    1968) (post-Mountbatten) is instructive. In the latter there is a substantial
    concern with management training, management review, and the appoint-
    ment of an industrial management consultant; whilst in the former such
    concerns are absent.
2. Although probation orders with requirements for supervision by a probation
    officer could not be made prior to the implementation of the 1907 Probation
    of Offenders Act, forms of probation were being used informally before that
    time using the binding over provisions of the 1879 Summary Jurisdiction
    Act. For an account see McWilliams (1986).
3. 'Dual control' was the system whereby the employees of voluntary societies
    were appointed as probation officers and thus were accountable both to their
    employers and to the courts which appointed them. The system was
    unsatisfactory and unpopular, but persisted until the late 1930s. For further
    details see Bochel (1976).
4. The idea of the probation service 'having a policy' is entirely modern. Before
    the Second World War when the newly-appointed Head of the Home Office
    Probation Branch, Mr B.J. Reynolds (1937) was asked about the future, he
    had no ideas other than getting on with the work in hand.
5. The total number of persons under the supervision of probation officers in
    England and Wales increased from 55,425 in 1951 to 90,459 in 1961 and to
    120,613 in 1971. The proportion of cases under after-care supervision
    increased from 10 per cent in 1951 to 14 per cent in 1961 and to 26 per cent
    in 1971. (See Probation and After-Care Statistics; Barr and O'Leary (1996);
    Home Office (1966b; 1969; 1972; 1976; 1979) and Department of
    Employment (1972)).
6. At least one probation area ignored the advice of the 1910 Departmental
    Committe and jumped the gun. On 15 April 1920 a sub-commitee of the
    justices in the City of Liverpool appointed Mr Harry Goldstone, a mission-
    ary officer of the Church of England Temperance Society, as 'chief proba-
    tion officer' for the city at an increased salary level.
7. For an example of this form of thought see Lacey (1991).
8. Another important area of practice in which principal probation officers were
    heavily involved was that of acting as liaison officers to courts of assize and
    quarter session. In the late 1960s roughly 70% of principal officers were thus
    involved, underlining the importance attached to the service's relationship
    with the courts. Today, not a single chief officer is liaison officer to a higher
    court, although the rhetoric of the value of close contacts with the courts
    remains in situ.
9. The idea that 'management is required to perform a planning and
    controlling function partly because of after-care work 'involving the use of
    volunteers' is incorrect. It is true that the Advisory Council on the
    Treatment of Offenders (Home Office 1963) had said that in the expanded
    probation and after-care service one of the principal probation officer's 'main

duties would be to enlist volunteers for personal service and to harness and stimulate the work of voluntary organisations' (para. 114), but the Advisory Council also said that this duty could be delegated. Delegated it was, and this was reinforced by a Home Office Circular (H.O.C. 144/1965) which suggested that the job could be 'more conveniently and effectively carried out by a local senior'.

10. See, for example, Lawrie (1989)

11. Strictly speaking, the intention was that offenders should be reformed, coercively if necessary, but the terms 'rehabilitation' and 'reformation' were regularly conflated in official pronouncements. For a discussion of why it is important to keep a clear distinction between the two see McWilliams and Pease (1990).

12. For a review of this argument and empirical evidence in this area see Fores and Sorge (1981).

13. Managers usually hold that procedure codes, practice handbooks, and so on are drawn up 'in consultation' with professional staff. This is frequently correct and its seems to strike an acceptable democratic note. However, being 'consulted' carries no guarantee of influence and I know of no empirical evidence to the effect that substantive changes regularly occur as a result of consultative exercises, despite the bureaucratic complexity which these often exhibit. Consultation is far removed from the model in which stakeholders in an organisation have a real say in its future direction.

14. My formulation of the situation specificity of practice action has been attacked by one chief probation officer (Lacey 1991) as 'indefensible, (p. 115). Perhaps I should emphasise that the point as made here is logical rather than empiricial.

15. For a valuable analysis of the modern social control school in penal thought see Peters (1986).

16. For an account of the key roles of critical appreciation and the critical culture see McWilliams (1989).

References

Allingham, L. (1975) 'Keeping on plodding', *Probation Journal*, 22, 73–76.

Ayscough, H. H. (1923) *When Mercy Seasons Justice: A Short History of the Work of the Church of England in the Police Courts*, Church of England Temperance Society.

Barr, H. and O'Leary, E. (1966) *Trends and Regional Comparisons in Probation (England and Wales)* Home Office Studies in the Causes of Delinquency and the Treatment of Offenders No.8, HMSO.

Bochel, D. (1976) *Probation and Aftercare: Its Development in England and Wales*, Scottish Academic Press.

Bottoms, A. E. and McWilliams, W. (1979) 'A non–treatment paradigm for probation practice', *BJSW*, 9, 159–202.

Colley, R. D., et al. (1970) 'Administration and individual responsibility', *Probation Journal*, 16, 86–88.

Department of Employment (1972) *Report of the Butterworth Inquiry into the Work and Pay of Probation Officers and Social Workers*, Cmnd 5076, HMSO.

Fores, M. and Sorge, A. (1981) 'The decline of the management ethic', *Journal of General Management*, Spring, 36–50.

Garland, D. (1990) *Punishment and Modern Society*, Oxford University Press.

Haxby, D. (1978) *Probation: A Changing Service*, Constable.

Hodgkinson, C. (1978) *Towards a Philosophy of Administration*, Blackwell.

Hodgkinson, C. (1983) *The Philosophy of Leadership*, Blackwell.

Home Office (1910a) *Report of the Departmental Committee on the Probation of Offenders Act*, 1907, CD 5001, HMSO.

Home Office (1910b) *Report of the Departmental Committee on the Probation of Offenders Act*, 1907, Minutes of Evidence, CD 5002, HMSO.

Home Office (1963) *The Organisation of Aftercare* (Report of the Advisory Council on the Treatment of Offenders), HMSO.

Home Office (1964) *Report of the Work of the Prison Department in the Year 1963*, Cmnd 2381, HMSO.

Home Office (1966a) *Report of the Inquiry into Prison Escapes and Security*, Cmnd 3175, HMSO.

Home Office (1966b) *Report on the Work of the Probation and Aftercare Department 1962–1965*, Cmnd 3107, HMSO.

Home Office (1968) *Report of the Work of the Prison Department 1967*, Cmnd 3774, HMSO.

Home Office (1969) *Report of the Work of the Probation and Aftercare Department 1966–1968*, Cmnd 4233, HMSO.

Home Office (1972) *Report of the Work of the Probation and Aftercare Department 1969–1971*, Cmnd 5158, HMSO.

Home Office (1976) *Report of the Work of the Probation and Aftercare Department 1972–1975*, Cmnd 6590, HMSO.

Home Office (1977) *A Review of Criminal Justice Policy 1976*, HMSO.

Home Office (1979) *Probation and Aftercare Statistics 1978*, HMSO.

Home Office and Lord Chancellor's Office (1961) *Report of the Interdepartmental Committee on the Business of the Criminal Courts*, Cmnd 1289, HMSO.

Home Office and Scottish Home Department (1962) *Report of the Departmental Committee on the Probation Service*, Cmnd 1650, HMSO.

Joint Negotiating Committee for the Probation Service (1980) Report of the *Working Party on Management Structure in the Probation and Aftercare Service*, JNC.

Lacey, M. (1991) 'The management ideal: a CPO's view', *Probation Journal*, 38, 110–117.

Lawrie, C. (1989) 'Management misunderstood' (letter), *Probation Journal*, 36, 48.

Lawless, D. (1989) 'The language of the grocer's shop', *The Tablet*, 20.5.89.

MacIntyre, A. (1981) *After Virtue: A Study in Moral Theory*, Duckworth.

McWilliams, W. (1981) 'The probation officer at court: from friend to acquaintance', *Howard Journal*, 20, 97–116.

McWilliams, W. (1986) 'The English Social Enquiry Report: development and practice', Ph.D. thesis, University of Sheffield, unpublished.

McWilliams, W. (1989) 'An expressive model for evaluating probation practice', *Probation Journal*, 36, 58–64.

McWilliams, W. and Pease, K. (1990) 'Probation practice and an end to punishment', *Howard Journal*, 29, 14–24.

National Association of Probation Officers (1970) *The Future Development of the Probation and Aftercare Service*, NAPO.

Peters, A.A.G.(1986) 'Main currents in criminal law theory in J.van Dijk, et al. (eds) *Criminal Law in Action*, Amham: Gouda Quint.

Potter, J. H. (1927) *Inasmuch: The Story of the Police Court Mission*, Williams and Norgate.

Principal Probation Officers' Conference (1968) *The Place of the Probation and Aftercare Service in Judicial Administration*, Leicester: PPOs Conference.

Reynold's, B. J. (1937) 'The future of the probation service', *Probation*, 2, 99–100.

Taylor, F. W. (1911) *The Principles of Scientific Management,* New York: Harper.
Temple, W. (1934) *The Ethics of Penal Action,* Clarke Hall Fellowship.
Thomas, C. (1978) 'Supervision in the Community', *Howard Journal,* 17, 23–31.
Walker, H. and Beaumont, B. (1981) *Probation Work: Critical Theory and Socialist Practice,* Macmillan.
Weston, W. R. (1973) 'Style of management in the probation and aftercare service', *Probation Journal,* 20, 69–73.
Whan, M. (1986) 'On the nature of practice', *BJSW,* 16, 243–50.

3 Towards managing the probation service

Roger Statham

Setting the scene

This chapter is devoted to a review of the factors influencing the development of management culture in the probation service during the 1980s and early 1990s. These are the views of one chief probation officer reflecting on the events of recent years and trying to make sense of them. The process is inevitably selective but it is intended to complement other contributions in this book and more particularly to stimulate thinking and debate.

It is difficult to define the genesis of management thinking in the probation service. To some extent it has always been there, initially enshrined in the roles of probation committees, and later manifested in the roles of principal and senior probation officers. But when the management grade grew and principals became chiefs, it was as much as anything a reflection of the growing size of the service, rather than a commitment to clear management ethic.

The service I joined in Stoke–on–Trent at the end of the 1960s was a loosely framed organisation with the accent very much on staff doing their own thing. The Probation Rules, various legislative Acts and Jarvis's Probation Officers' Manual (Weston, 1987) seemed to be the only authorities. It is perhaps worth remembering though that the role of the Home Office was influential in maintaining and developing service culture through its training role and its control over the confirmation process. The Home Office training structure placed a heavy emphasis on probation practice, and both the professional and direct entry courses contributed to a sense of identity and provided continuity.

It is also worth remembering that the service was much smaller; the principal probation officer's conference was the major management think tank and everybody belonged to the National Association of Probation Officers (NAPO). The debates in the late 1960s, post–Seebohm (1968), had produced a growing awareness of social work professionalism and although probation officers decided they did not want to join social workers, they quickly decided that they wanted their training. The optimism of the 1960s was reflected in the development of the treatment model (Whitehead, 1990), analogous in the medical metaphor. At the day to day practical level senior probation officers were professional advisors and administrative structures were minimal. For the probation officer there was a tremendous sense of freedom to practice because structures were loose and supervision was not intrusive in terms of either quantity or quality. Furthermore evaluations, when they were produced, were often unseen by recipients and were thus a low key affair. It is perhaps worth remembering that many of today's chief probation officers served their apprenticeship in this era.

This brief scene setting is merely an attempt to provide some insight into how the service was. There is no thorough attempt to analyse this historical scenario, but it will serve as a marker against which to gauge reflection about change.

Management culture – some early signs

There have been many significant events in the development of management culture in the probation service and my starting point is community service which has had a major impact on probation management. Community service, the brainchild of the Wootton Committee set up by a socialist regime in 1966, posed new managerial challenges for the service when it was finally implemented through the 1972 Criminal Justice Act. The sentence of community service required the working off of hours in a practical work orientated setting. Systems had to be devised for the monitoring of hours and structures developed to ensure work was available and completed in a satisfactory way. New expertise and skills had to be developed. This significant innovation was left to a small group of senior probation officers, generally known as community service organisers, who were charged with developing the management skills necessary to make the system work. It was an era of pioneering and inventiveness, which was to prove that the probation service could handle operations outside the traditional casework structure. It says much for the qualities of those within the service that it was done without much formal input from the Home Office whose training input was less than adequate.

Within the service criticisms of community service reflected concerns about the erosion of social work values and brought complaints about coercion. The premise that making offenders do things against their will, as it was suggested community service did, was thought to be the thin end of the penal wedge and as such was ideologically unsound. Equally, supporters of the scheme believed that potential for rehabilitation and reformation existed alongside reparation. Moreover there was a recognition that this new sentence promoted understanding of crime within the community and offered the potential for partnership.

The development of management skills such as budgeting, target setting, public relations, monitoring and referral systems, became essential. The acquisition of projects and sessional staff were part of a range of new skills which in turn were part of the new agenda for partnership. The important skill to develop was budgeting and a swathe of new middle managers found themselves preoccupied with the issue of financial management. During the mid 1970s, which witnessed the problems of the three day week, community service was competing for scarce resources. However, community service organisers had to make bids for more resources, having achieved targets, targets which were usually expressed as numbers of new orders. Here was a simple resource related management model, because the achievement of numerical targets became part of a process of justifying existing resources and bidding successfully for more. Community service also heralded other changes because probation officers had to begin to think more widely about sentencing options. Now using both hostels and community service they had, in fact, become brokers of resources.

In the context of the development of management skills another more subtle change was taking place. As senior probation officers moved out of community service and back into fieldwork units, they took their newly acquired skills with them. Through this continuing process there was a growing group of managers in the service who had developed a latent management potential, and who had begun to perceive their role in a very different way than that of the traditional casework consultant senior probation officer. In community service issues such as monitoring workloads, managing resources and perhaps more importantly monitoring the attendance of offenders and breaching for non–attendance, had been part of every day practice. Furthermore, community service had such a high public relations profile with the courts that there was a real sense of a growing understanding of the expectations of sentencers.

The influence of the market at the end of the 1970s brought about by a change of government, produced a new agenda for the public sector. The philosophy of the market began to impose itself on the thinking of public service agencies through the actions of a government with a clear market driven philosophy and a commitment to impose its dogma. The report of the Efficiency Unit in 1985 reflected a firm commitment to follow this process through. The British government was not alone in making this shift. Most western governments and their economies have been similarly influenced, with perhaps the most staggering changes occurring in eastern Europe at the end of the 1980s and beginning of the 1990s.

It would not be appropriate to turn this into an economics paper, the author's knowledge would preclude it anyway, but it is probably helpful to dwell for a moment on market thinking. Visionaries like Toffler (1971) had begun to predict the impact of new technology on the world. Manufacturing industries as part of their need for survival have adopted increasingly automated/ robotic means of production. New technology has become both a means of ensuring quality control and increasing output. Thus the idiosyncrasies of the human performance dimension of production have been increasingly controlled and fewer people have been employed. New technology has also improved communication and goods can be transported more quickly and easily. This technology provides an opportunity for tight stock control, which in itself decreases overheads and increases competitiveness. These changes have enabled manufacturing bases to be spread and components can be manufactured widely and assembled centrally. Furthermore traditional skills are not always essential in setting up new operations. As a result, major manufacturers have become multinational corporations, exploiting cheaper options in a process of manufacturing globalisation. As a consequence, some traditional industrial countries have begun to experience deficits in trade balances. They have become poorer and because of this have less to spend on their infrastructures. This, in turn, puts pressure on public services. It is difficult to separate the market/ economic influence from political thinking, but as Statham (1990) suggests 'it was inconceivable that the public sector would be left untouched by the pace of change in the business world'(p.4).

The market world thinking seems to have impacted on the work of the probation service in three ways. Firstly, as a direct consequence of the new agenda for public sector management epitomised by the Efficiency Unit and its value for money language. As management concepts developed through manufacturing industry were imported into the service, there were inevitably going to be tensions concerning concepts and language. Secondly, market dogma also brought with it expectations of competition at a personal level which had an impact on attitudes in society generally. Thirdly, economic considerations were used to implement harsh social policy changes which underlined the divisiveness of the social structure and clearly disadvantaged the groups with which the service was engaged.

The impact of government thinking

Faced with restrictions on revenue all governments have difficult decisions to make about priorities in public sector spending. The policies pursued by the Conservatives in the 1980s are interesting. The industrial base was in decline, new technology had reduced the workforce and unemployment was rising. Alternative revenue was generated through profits from the oil industry and by privatising public utilities. This was a strategy to generate significant amounts of extra short term money for the exchequer, The resulting revenue was used as an opportunity for the government to begin to reduce direct taxation to fulfil election promises. Higher rates of tax were reduced significantly and the basic rate of taxation came down to twenty–five pence in the pound. These policies increased the proportionate wealth of the top few per cent of the population.

Simultaneously the government was pursuing a rigorous policy with regard to expenditure on social security benefits. With an ageing population and exceptionally high rates of unemployment the number dependent on state benefit increased significantly. Consequently the government has tried to encourage the expansion of private pension provision through various incentives. At the same time claiming benefit has become more difficult and some, like child benefit, has not kept pace with inflation. Studies like Empty Rooms (Cleveland County Council, 1991) have clearly illustrated the widening poverty gap and the fact that relative deprivation has increased significantly during the 1980s.

Probation officers in their day–to–day work are very much in touch with the impact of government social policy. Unemployment in the North–East (Statham et al., 1987) underlined the impact of unemployment within probation caseloads. This piece of work not only made links between unemployment and crime, it also highlighted the issue of poverty. This prompted further work to be done on the issue of poverty in Cleveland (Leishman et al., 1989) and also stimulated the Association of Chief Officers of Probation (ACOP) into commissioning research. Surviving Poverty (ACOP, 1989) illustrated the financial difficulties of probationers and other offenders under supervision. Halmos (1978) identified the tension between the personal and political aspects of social work. Social policy decisions taken during the 1980s increased perceptions of social injustice and provided a fertile breeding ground within the probation service for disaffection with the government and its policies. The government's record on tax cuts in itself would, in the minds of most probation officers, have been an unacceptable alternative to the challenge of redirecting some of the money from the pockets of the wealthy to essential social policy initiatives, like poverty, unemployment, health and education.

Interestingly whilst the probation service was in its day–to–day work experiencing the impact of poverty, as a result of social policy decisions, it was at the same time receiving significant extra resources from government. During the 1980s the probation service increased in size from 5602 in 1980 to 6967 probation officers in 1989 (an increase of 24%). Ironically it was probably this growth and their lack of control over it which provided the genesis for the government's plan for cash limiting the probation service which started to impact during 1992. It is worth remembering that this cash–limiting strategy for controlling public expenditure had been used in the health service and department of social security. Recognising the results of this and the threats of these measures being used in probation helped to increase the disaffection of probation officers with government policy. Against this background service managers found themselves having to respond to expectations of managing which were increasingly dictated by business world thinking and the dynamics of the market.

The challenge of management

Against this background the probation service began to embark on a new era of management in a situation in which the work force could readily identify these initiatives with a government with which it had little sympathy. It can safely be argued that probation officers have a legitimate lobby in the context of social policy. In making the complex links between poverty, unemployment, deprivation and crime, the service is able to articulate the weaknesses of a criminal justice policy which ignores the impact of social policy decisions. This was particularly true in the 1980s when the probation service was being urged to take on more high risk offenders in the community. At the same time for so many offenders life could only promise unemployment and poverty, factors which many probation officers would argue contribute to criminal and other perceived anti–social activities.

With hindsight perhaps not enough effort was made by the probation service to exploit the opportunity of its lobby potential. Perhaps if more had been made of this, influence on government might have been more effective. Reasons for it not happening are perhaps due to the disparate nature of the then fifty–six probation areas, and perhaps the wider preoccupations of both ACOP and NAPO. However, because of the lack of coordinated lobby activity it was perhaps easy for the workforce to see the growth of management in the service as a response to the demands of an uncaring government, rather than a legitimate exercise in ensuring the careful use of diminishing public resources.

Questioning the need of management

Another dimension of the development of management in probation stems from the history and culture of the service itself. The points made at the beginning of this chapter are perhaps worth more reflection. In the *laissez faire* culture of the past any management was bound to be seen as onerous. The rapid imposition of so–called industrial techniques could only have been experienced as earth–shattering. Resistance was to be expected, not only from the point of view of the experience of individuals within the service, but also in terms of the objectives of an increasingly iconoclastic NAPO whose anti–management stance was encapsulated in its policy of seniorless teams which it pursued during the 1980s. Some of the tensions associated with developing management culture have been explored within the *Probation Journal*. McWilliams (1990) argued against the need for management which he saw as manipulative and perhaps coercive. Instead he argued in favour of the ideal of probation practice suggesting that 'excellence in practice is to be had only through the exercise of justice, courage and honesty' (1990, p.61). He goes on to articulate a management model which relates the monitoring of standards to an inspection process deemed in itself to be non–manipulative. The model also differentiates between formal accountability and substantive accountability. The former a means by which organisations correct procedures and then consequently inhibit risk taking and diminish personal responsibility; the latter a process by which it is possible when errors occur 'for individuals to take the lessons of events into their hearts and into their practice' (p.67). McWilliam's views have to be taken seriously and as a contributor to the management debate he is to be found within this book.

In responding to some of his ideas it has to be conceded that it is difficult to claim that the management process can be morally neutral. However, it is possible to put alternative interpretations on some of the issues raised. For example, the development of policy designed to control offending has not replaced traditional concern for individual offenders. Equally organisational excellence is not simply about the promotion of manipulation, it is about the very issue of practice excellence he espouses. Perhaps the real problem lies within the contemporary nature of current management thinking within the probation service. The acquisition of industrial management thinking is perhaps still a little too bald and has yet to be adapted to fit the nature of the probation operation. However, this process will happen and the present debate is an essential part of the evolutionary process. Whatever the merits of McWilliam's arguments because they are, on the face of it, anti–management, they find sympathy amongst some staff within the probation service. It is very easy for the probation workforce to see the government's aspirations for Punishment, Custody and the Community (Home Office, 1988a) as a recipe for coercion. Although in reality it must be fair to say that no one in the probation service believes that offenders can be coerced into a therapeutic relationship. Equally it would have to be conceded that probation supervision has never been control free. Indeed Lacey (1991) asserts the intrinsic nature of social control within the work of the probation service.

I would argue that probation officers, in discharging their duties, have always had to combine support for the individual with the control expected of them in their position within the criminal justice system. Advise, assist and befriend may have always been open to differing interpretations but there was never a place for radical non–intervention.

The key to McWilliam's position lies in the notions of substantive accountability. This being a process by which the hearts and presumably the minds of probation officers are influenced in a way which affects their practice. This concept reinforces the view of the probation service as a group of self–regulating professionals, striving continuously to achieve excellence. Sadly this is not always the case and so both inspection and supervision are designed to give insights into and influence performance. Subsequently judgements have to be made about performance at two levels. Firstly, at a practical level which concerns the organising of work, use of time and deciding priorities. Secondly, as an exploration of the working relationship between probation officer and offender. In the first situation some assessment would have to be made about the organisational and personal management skills of the individual officer. The second would require an assessment of social work skills and the ability to develop effective working relationships with offenders.

A legitimate aspiration for the management process, therefore, is to assess and influence performance and create a climate for the development of excellence. This notion might fly in the face of probation officer autonomy, but the claim to autonomy is based on a false premise of independence. Probation officers are part of a formal organisation in which there are expectations of performance which is influenced by its position in the criminal justice system. Furthermore the magistracy played an important part in the setting up of the probation service. They, along with other sentencers, have always had expectations of how the service conducts its supervision of offenders. Lacey (1991) in his reflection on policy and power, articulates some of the arguments. One of the inherent tensions for probation officers is that they have a range of expectations to meet. Apart from the boundaries provided by statute; the Courts as the major customer; the Home Office, the Local Authority and the public, all significant stakeholders, have expectations too. These expectations relate to the performance of probation officers and their crucial place with the criminal justice system. Put simply, probation practice has to address the issue of crime because this is precisely what the probation service is paid to do. But the task should be undertaken with compassion and traditional values, represented in the history and culture of the service.

In a sense the probation service is at a point of tension in the criminal justice system, having to absorb the negativism and despair transferred to it by its consumers (offenders), whilst maintaining the confidence of its customers (the Courts) and major stakeholders (the Home Office, Local Authority and community). Service management has an essential part to play in helping develop strategies for absorbing these tensions, ensuring continued confidence in service performance and perhaps even lobbying for change. These stresses will not be easy to handle. For example it will be easy and quite natural for the needs of the individual offender to be championed by probation staff. But this simply cannot be done without attention paid to the offending behaviour of that same individual. Thus the management process again has a part to play in ensuring that practice is secure. Furthermore, whilst in theory the self regulating member of staff will cope without the support and guidance of a manager, in reality practice has been far too patchy for too long for this to be taken for granted. The courts, as customers, are aware of this because, for example, the quality of social inquiry reports is variable and links will be made between these and other aspects of service performance. Questions are now being asked about service performance and this will be an increasing trend in an era of inspection and national standards.

Another dimension was added to management by the Beckford Report (1985). The climate in which the work was done reflected fundamental dilemmas in social work and of its supervision by managerial staff. Supervision is essentially critical analysis and as a process affords protection to both the probation officer/social worker and the recipient of the service. When social work practice is exposed in such critical areas of practice as child protection, and the supervision of high risk offenders in the community, it seems unfair and unwise to leave practice entirely to the hands of individual notions of good standards.

Questioning management style and processes seems to be both relevant and necessary against such a background. A management ideal for the probation service may be impossible to define at this point in time, and in the context of the transient nature of things may never be achieved. However, it would not seem to be a question of whether we manage but how. Arguments against management seem set to founder simply because of inconsistency of performance. The ideal of a totally self–regulating workforce is beyond social work, just as it eludes other organisations which means that management is essential to ensure both quality and consistency of service delivery. The issues, therefore, are about the nature and quality of management.

Greater accountability

Throughout much of the 1980s and into the 1990s the probation service has been subjected to direct government influence through the Home Office and other bodies. The onslaught of initiatives and directives has not so much influenced but rather driven management thinking and processes. The statement of National Objectives and Priorities (SNOP) (Home Office, 1984b) clearly set out the Home Office view of the probation service. The letter accompanying the document contained key paragraphs:

> The statement is a Home Office document, but one which we
> believe will command a large measure of support from the

probation service. It sets out for the first time the Home Office
view of the purpose of the probation service, the specific tasks
which it should undertake and the broad order of priorities
which it should follow. During the next few months the
Probation Inspectorate will be seeking discussion with
committees and Chief Officers about priorities and the
resources to be devoted to particular activities in each area
Service. I am sure that you will be ready to respond positively
to this approach (Faulkner, 1984, p. 1–2).

SNOP began to talk of efficient and effective use of resources.
It went on to define the purpose, objectives and priorities of the
probation service in language that was new and consequences
enormous. The probation service was located within a criminal
justice system and the confidence of the community highlighted.
The role of the service in courts was reinforced as was the supervision of offenders subject to various facets of community supervision. Other aspects of the service's work, like throughcare and
civil work, were seen to be less important. Local probation areas
were later asked to produce their own local statements of objectives and priorities which ushered in changes that can only be
described as profound. The language being used was that of
business management and the basic management by objective
approach was reinforced by the Home Office's promotion of
Gilpin Black and other firms of management consultants.
Effectiveness seminars were provided by the Home Office for
senior managers, who were then encouraged to buy–in this
expertise as part of a process of developing an in–house management culture. Probation committees played an important part in
these developments by formally approving local statements of
objectives and priorities.

Furthermore, the Grimsey Report (Home Office, 1987) was an
efficiency scrutiny of the Inspectorate. This report directly related
to the government's efficiency unit initiative and was to have a
major impact on the Inspectorate and the service as a whole. Not
only did it change the size and structure of the Inspectorate but it
also refocussed its work in a major way. It also had far reaching
implications for the work of the service. For example the need for
practice guidelines was spelled out. The full implications of this
report will not be felt until well into the 1990s.

Following Grimsey, desk top inspections were carried out by
the Inspectorate on all probation areas during 1988, using previously determined performance indicators. In 1989 ten areas
were selected for efficiency and effectiveness inspections as part of
an ongoing programme. Efficiency and Effectiveness Inspection in

the Probation Service (HM Inspectorate of Probation, 1990) was a report of this first year of the inspection programme. The summary of main conclusions included:

2.2.   Inspection visits to the ten selected areas found that impressive progress was being made in the management of the service at area level, defining policies, setting objectives and preparing practice guidelines. There was still some confusion, however, about management concepts and terminology and in setting precise objectives and targets for work lower down the organisation.

2.5   Changes in the Criminal Justice System and the development of specialisation within the probation service required greater clarity and some reassessment of the roles of the CPO, ACPO, SPO, particularly in delegating responsibility, holding staff to account and judging performance in terms of results achieved rather than good intentions.

2.8   As an interim measure there was need to explore systems whereby managers at all levels could receive information about the cost of their decisions. No area was found where expenditure was coded and information available on a regular basis for expenditure on each team and type of work (p.4).

This document also reinforced the need for better information systems and there was a section on terminology and congruence with government policy and we can see that the message of SNOP was implemented through the Grimsey scrutiny. The impact of these measures was considerable and reinforced clear expectations about the way in which the service should be managed.

By late 1989 the probation service was receiving attention more widely, both from the National Audit Office and the Audit Commission. The National Audit Office report (1989) commented on the structure and organisation of the service in great detail. It also gave reinforcement to common objectives; better targeting of service delivery; and as might have been expected, improving economy, efficiency and effectiveness.

Subsequently the Audit Commission report 'The Probation Service: Promoting Value For Money' (1989a) was followed by an audit exercise which was intended to involve all probation areas. With one or two exceptions this process is now complete. For the purposes of the audit a guide was produced which contained 241 pages (Audit Commission, 1989b). Auditors, either from private practice or district audit offices duly arrived and, using the guide, produced reports that were presented to probation committees.

The whole exercise was an in–depth look at probation area operations. Whilst it was a further reinforcement of the 3 Es and value for money, the focus of the audits was very much on management processes within areas. The audit process was not an entirely comfortable one and the cultural differences between the traditional position of the probation service in the criminal justice system was challenged when it was suggested that the service deal with more serious offenders. There seems to be a clear perception here that the probation service can influence the sentencing process. Whilst this may be too bald a statement for comfort, the expectations of government are being clearly reiterated.

Following the audits of 1990 the Audit Commission produced an occasional paper titled 'Going Straight: Developing Good Practice in the Probation Service' (1991). The paper contained a reminder that auditors had left behind them action plans for implementation in all areas, and that progress would be monitored from year to year. It also reinforced the services major objective which, according to the Audit Commission, is to reduce offending. It has to be said that it is a bold, if not breathtaking objective. Its simplicity could be interpreted as mind boggling, inspirational or naive. But the inevitable 'how' question is not answered. One response to this objective would be to say that surely we could not ignore social policy factors in offending or as an essential part of the reformative process. As the probation service does not have control over all these factors, success cannot be guaranteed. Nevertheless the challenge remains. In Audit Commission terms the service will have to demonstrate effectiveness, which is about having an effect on offending behaviour.

The report goes on to state that the new criminal justice legislation will have a profound effect on probation and the criminal justice system, but interestingly, other comments trace a link back to 1984. The overall impression from the audit reports is that the service should continue to develop a more managerial approach.

In continuing this theme of greater accountability it is important to look at the role of the Probation Division (C6) within the Home Office. In 1989 there was a specific initiative on 17–20 year old offenders, who were identified as a key target group. Chief officers were requested to produce specific action plans to deal with this group and plans were required to be forwarded to the Home Office for scrutiny (Home Office, 1988b). The increasingly influential role of the Probation Division can be seen in the growth of 'Dear CPO' letters because during 1990 chief probation officers received forty–two of these. Some were more important than others and whilst not attempting to assess the complexity of each one the sheer weight in numbers illustrates the determination of the department to influence the work of the service.

Probation service training has also been reviewed. The Coleman report (Home Office, 1989) reviewed facilities for professional training for probation officers. This was followed by a scrutiny of in–service training arrangements in 1991 (Home Office, 1991a). It is not easy to gauge the impact of either or both of these exercises. However, in the context of other events impacting on the service and the rapid pace of change, the former might have produced a strategy for detaching probation training from main stream social work. It did not and largely satisfied itself with recommendations about the content and quality of future training. The implications of the in–service training scrutiny have yet to be fully felt, but there are indications that management training is to have a slightly higher profile.

There are further major initiatives which need to be reviewed in this section on accountability. The first of these is national standards. As indicated earlier the Grimsey report identified a need for national standards because of a perceived lack of objective criteria against which performance might be judged. The programme of developing national standards began in 1989 with community service (Home Office, 1988c). By 1991 national standards were being developed for probation supervision (Home Office, 1991b), pre–sentence reports (Home Office, 1991b) and combination orders (Home Office, 1991c). All these documents, and others to follow, will have a major influence on service practice and will be monitored by the Home Office. The pre–sentence report document probably represents the most significant change in probation practice. The work of years developing professional practice in report writing will be encapsulated in a new coherent format for these reports. There will also be provision for a quick response to court deadlines, and the contentious issue of recommendations will finally be dealt with.

The precise impact and outcomes of these three new documents cannot be fully anticipated at this stage, but it is clear that the Home Office wants the work on combination orders and pre–sentence reports completed before the implementation of the 1991 Criminal Act in October 1992. The timescale for response to these important documents, two months, is also part of the new management agenda of accountability.

Another important part of this agenda is the development of the Resource Management Information System (RMIS) for the probation service. The idea began as a financial management initiative for the probation service and its development is well documented by Humphrey (1987). A great deal of work had been undertaken by the end of the 1980s and by the beginning of the 1990s it looks as though the service will have this resource tool by 1993/1994. The capacity of RMIS to go beyond efficiency measures into effectiveness measures is questionable. Furthermore the degree of sophistication of both information and local authority finance systems will be an important factor for many areas.

It could be argued that the most fundamental change for the service will be the implementation of cash limits in April 1992. Although a good deal of preparatory work has been done during 1990 and 1991 there is still much more to learn about operational impact. Many probation areas will have difficulty in effectively monitoring finance. Traditional links with local authority treasurers have not provided the quality of financial information necessary to achieve the sophistication now required. Consequently there is much work to do to ensure financial systems work well and this could lead to increased development of in–house systems.

In turning to the operational implications of a cash limited budget there is clearly much to learn. The safety net has been removed and areas must now manage and make some uncomfortable decisions about priorities. In view of the many developments associated with the Criminal Justice Act 1991 and the extra demands of national standards, these decisions will become even more acute. It is probably impossible to undertake an exercise of this size and complexity without criticism. But there must always be legitimate doubts about the capacity of any cash limit formula to get it right (Home Office, 1991d). Nevertheless the detail of the cash limit circulars (Home Office, 1991d and Home Office, 1991e) reinforces the accountability of local probation areas. Whilst cash limits will clearly be a major part of the new accountability, the Home Office Blue Paper decision document (Home Office, 1991f) is interesting in that it cements all the recent initiatives together. It also suggests that the changes are not complete. The implications of this document are far reaching and spell out the government's intentions to:

- ensure responsiveness to national objectives and standards

- clarify accountabilities and responsibilities

- improve the effectiveness of management

- increase the confidence of sentencers in the probation service

- encourage high standards of practice

- improve working relationships with other agencies and organisations

- encourage and strengthen the links between the probation service and the local community.

To facilitate these the Government will consult on:

- the restructuring of committees
- criteria for amalgamation of probation services
- arrangements for regional collaboration
- arrangements for liaison with sentencers
- arrangements for co–operation between the prison and probation services.

On the face of it another exhausting list of changes.

This section on accountability has been superficial and may also be seen as a crude review of what has been happening to the probation service over recent years. Nevertheless, what it has done, I hope, is to convey something of the growing demands of accountability being placed on the service and the accompanying need for management to ensure accountability.

Some of the implications

The great challenge for the probation service is to make sense of the process which began with SNOP in 1984 and has now reached the stage of cash limits in 1992. Some process of reflection is now needed to put events into perspective and to understand their implications. Whilst there will be no consensus, and perhaps the real solutions will appear with the benefit of hindsight, it is important that the issues relating to the future of the service are engaged with. One of the difficulties for many working within the probation service is that recent initiatives flow from the new right doctrines of the Tory government elected in 1979. The ideology of this government, epitomised by its reiteration of individual responsibility and commitment to the competition of the market, will not be readily embraced by an organisation whose roots are embedded in a tradition of caring for the individual. There will be those who would wish events would go away or equally might prefer to ignore them. The flight to the *laissez faire* environment described above may seem compelling.

Much of what has been happening has concerned the process of developing management. Whilst there will be those like McWilliams (1990) who will argue about whether it is needed in the probation service, it does look as though it is here to stay. Events reviewed in this chapter and elsewhere in this book would seem to suggest a certain inevitability. One of the problems at this point in time is trying to make sense of the language and thinking of industrial management and relating them to the probation service. Perhaps we should accept that this process is going to take time and that we will not get it right easily or quickly. I would argue, however, that there is much to be gained by developing an appropriate management culture in the service. Certainly it is not easy to argue that the service has always been efficient and although effectiveness measures are notoriously difficult to define, the most positive gloss will not hide the shortcomings in practice. A well managed service will be part of ensuring that performance is always convincing.

Thomas (1990) raised a number of issues about practice, citing that in a sample of 600 cases from ten probation areas, over half were seen fortnightly or less in the first three months. Of the findings Thomas goes on to say 'they suggest that in a significant number of cases neither the public nor the individual offender may have been receiving the sort of service they were entitled to expect'. Thomas makes other important points about the credibility of the service in his paper. Points about quality being about giving offenders time, 'being seen regularly, having issues dealt with, the order focused and rigorously enforced' (p. 11) are difficult to argue with. The probation service must not react to this criticism in a defensive way and it should be acknowledged that targets and objectives set for areas of work over which the service has no control, like sentencing, are unachievable. Nevertheless, the service has the responsibility to devise objectives and targets more appropriate to its work and Thomas's observations about levels of contact cannot be ignored. Levels of contact are a major professional issue, directly related to service values. Put simply no contact means no care. Consistency in practice standards is not a knee jerk response to the political agenda but is about the service's confidence in its own ability to promote the primacy of its role in the criminal justice system. The political reality is about the recognition that without change the service may not be able to hold onto its traditional monopoly.

Therefore, the message is clear. The probation service's major stakeholder, the Home Office, which supplies 80% and more of the service's funding and which is in a unique position constitutionally, is determined to push through changes. It would be easy to think of management as a novelty, as something imposed on the service for the sake of change. In my view this would be to misinterpret events since 1984. Management is now firmly on the agenda and is a legitimate innovation in the service's history. The challenge is now to develop a style of management relevant to the service. In the short term this will mean adopting the concepts and language of industrial commercial management.

Crucially, the lead must come from senior managers which can be facilitated by the ACOP structure which provides a real opportunity. A forward looking strategy is now needed which takes account of the structures and constraints, but which articulates the service's own vision of the future which uses the richness of its formidable experience of the criminal justice system.

References

Association of Chief Officers of Probation (1989) *Surviving Poverty:Probation Work and Benefit Policy*, Lancaster University.

Audit Commission (1989a) *The Probation Service: Promoting Value for Money*, HMSO.

Audit Commission (1989b) *Probation Audit Guide*, HMSO.

Audit Commission (1991) *Going Straight: Developing Good Practice in the Probation Service*, HMSO, Occasional Paper.

Beckford Report (1985) *A Child in Trust*, Kingswood Publications.

Cleveland County Council (1991) *Empty Rooms*.

Efficiency Unit (1985) *Making Things Happen*, HMSO.

Faulkner, D. E. R. (1984) Letter accompanying SNOP, Home Office.

Grimsey, E. J. (1987) *Efficiency Scrutiny of the Probation Inspectorate*, Home Office.

Halmos, P. (1978) *The Personal and the Political*, Constable.

HM Inspectorate of Probation (1990) *Efficiency and Effectiveness Inspection in the Probation Service: The First Year*, Home Office.

Home Office (1984a) *The Probation Rules*, Cmd 647, HMSO.

Home Office (1984b) *Probation Service in England and Wales: Statement of National Objectives and Priorities*, HMSO.

Home Office (1987) *See* Grimsey above.

Home Office (1988a) *Punishment, Custody and the Community*, Cmd 424, HMSO.

Home Office (1988b) *Tackling Offending: An Action Plan*, HMSO.

Home Office (1988c) *National Standards for Community Service Orders*, HMSO.

Home Office (1989) *Probation Training: Review of Home Office Sponsorship Scheme, (the Coleman Report)*, HMSO.

Home Office (1991a) *Report of a Scrutiny of Probation in-service Training*, HMSO.

Home Office (1991b) *Pre-sentence Reports*, CPO 46/1991, HMSO.

Home Office (1991c) *Combination Orders*, CPO 47/1991, HMSO.

Home Office (1991d) *Cash Limits*, CPO 44/1991, HMSO.

Home Office (1991e) *Cash Limits*, CPO 23/1991, HMSO.

Home Office (1991f) *Organising Supervision and Punishment in the Community*, Blue paper Discussion Document, HMSO.

Humphrey, C. (1987) *The Implications of the Financial Management Initiative for the Probation Service*, University of Manchester.

Lacey, M. (1991) The Management Ideal: A CPO's view. *Probation Journal*, 38, 3.

Leishman, J., Biddle, D. and Whitehead, P (1989) *Case Studies in Poverty*, Cleveland Probation Service.

McWilliams, W. (1990) 'Probation practice and the management ideal', *Probation Journal*, 37, 2.

National Audit Office (1989) *Home Office Control and Management of Probation Services in England and Wales*, HMSO.

Seebohm (1968) *Report of the Committee on Local Authority and Personal Social Services*, Cmd 3703, HMSO.

Statham, R. S. (1987) *Unemployment in the North–East* ACOP.

Statham, R. S. (1990) *The Probation Service in a market driver world*, Cleveland Probation Service.

Thomas, C. (1990) *A Proper Curiosity: IMI in Context*, Home Office.

Toffler, A (1971) *Future Shock*, Pan.

Toren, N. (1972) *Social Work: The case for a Senior Profession*, Sage.

Weston, W. R. (1987) *Jarvis's Probation Officers' Manual*, 4th edn, Butterworth.

Whitehead, P. (1990) *Community Supervision for Offenders*, Avebury.

Wootton, B. (1970) *Advisory Committee on the Penal System: Non–custodial and semi–custodial sentences*, HMSO.

4 Managing the future

Roger Statham

This chapter explores some of the factors in managing the probation service of the future. As such it will articulate some of the issues and choices facing the service which will provide a contrast to some of the other ideas expressed in this book, whilst making discernible links with others.

In making the connection with the previous chapter, I want to argue that the comprehensive agenda for change, reinforced by the Home Office since the Statement of Objectives and Priorities in 1984, has created the need for specific thinking about management. I will not rehearse the arguments behind this supposition again, but merely content myself with saying that the developments of the last twenty years have left the service resembling the ideal type 'professional bureaucracy' articulated by Mintzberg (1983) who says that

> The Professional Bureaucracy is unique among the five configurations in answering two of the paramount needs of contemporary men and women. It is democratic, disseminating its power directly to its workers (at least those who are professional). And it provides them with extensive autonomy, freeing them even of the need to coordinate closely with their peers and all the pressures and politics that entails. Thus, the professional has the best of both worlds: he is attached to an organisation, yet is free to serve his clients in his own way, constrained only by the established standards of his profession (p. 205).

Mintzberg goes on to suggest that this kind of organisation allows professionals to perfect their skills free from interference. However, there are also problems with this kind of structure for there is virtually no control of the work except by the profession itself and no way to correct deficiencies the professionals themselves choose to overlook (p. 206). Two other important points are made. The professional bureaucracy cannot easily deal with professionals who are either incompetent or unconscientious and discretion not only enables some professionals to ignore the needs of their clients but it also encourages many of them to ignore the needs of the organisation. Mintzberg's idea is that of a loosely framed organisation which leaves the quality of service delivery in the hands of practitioners. There has been an aspiration that this loose kind of organisation would be the means by which innovation was promoted and best practice secured. However, the Home Office report on Efficiency and Effectiveness (HM Inspectorate of Probation, 1990) has challenged these assumptions. Whilst there are clear examples of excellent practice, performance is patchy and variable. These insights into practice illustrate some of the problems articulated by Mintzberg and present chief probation officers and other senior managers with the responsibility of responding and subsequently of articulating how they might achieve the practice ideals to which they aspire. This can be facilitated by the creation of a management culture, but to say this may generate language problems which, therefore, should be addressed.

There are barriers to the language of objectives, targets and performance indicators currently being used within the service. This is probably because these terms are more readily identified with efficiency measures than effectiveness and quality. Efficiency is not a concept with which the service is familiar and is unlikely to immediately gladden the hearts of an organisation which has a history devoted to ideals of caring and compassion, hidden from the glare of financial accountability. But the world has changed. Perhaps the service would do well to remind itself that all public services, both statutory and voluntary, have similar traditions and caring values. However, this has not been the means of escaping scrutiny of performance or economic reality, as those in health, education and the citizen's advice bureau, will testify. I will return later to the question of language because at this point other issues should be touched upon which in my view cannot be avoided.

What kind of service is being provided? What is the service in business for? Are the probation service's customers and consumers, the courts and the offenders, satisfied with the quality of service being offered? Are the right kind of services being made available? What is the service trying to achieve? How does it measure its achievements? What processes, systems and strategies are needed in developing effective probation management?

How to respond

Acknowledging the inevitable differences of fifty–five probation areas underlines the problems of any kind of cohesive response or action to the questions posed. Whilst there does seem to be some sense of corporate national identity as well as local area identity, it is nevertheless difficult for the service to muster an effective and consistent response to criminal justice issues, government initiatives, or indeed management issues. As a consequence it is easy to perceive the service as simply reacting to the agendas of others and in the probation service this means drifting towards a future manufactured by the Home Office. As always there is an antidote to this negative scenario which lies in the potential of a proactive organisation responding to the many challenges. For example the Association of Chief Officers of Probation (ACOP) was going through a fairly major metamorphosis during 1991. It may yet emerge as a coordinating force with the potential to be able to answer some of the questions and to contribute to the development of a management culture that could deliver quality services. The key to this process is understanding, which sounds simple enough. But ultimately it requires a total workforce understanding of what the service should deliver and of the management systems and strategies necessary to ensure achievement.

For this to begin to happen there has to be some clarity about where the service fits into the criminal justice system. Perhaps because of the endless arguments about welfare versus control, which seem to have moved the service psyche towards pure welfare over the past twenty years, there was inevitably a reaction of horror in some quarters to Home Office thinking on punishment in the community. So what is the probation services role in the criminal justice system? There has been no shortage of commentators who have attempted to define this over the years, but I think it is fair to say that there is no generally held view and perhaps there never will be a consensus. But an organisation which is not clear about its purpose must be open to fragmentation even beyond Handy's (1985) perceptions of organisational life. Tuck (1989) suggested that the work of the service was underpinned by four main principles: the probation service is about dealing with offenders as defined by the courts; enforcing the orders of the courts, within powers delegated by statute; to maximise chances of not re–offending against the criminal law; helping offenders to become functioning members of a free community (p.139–140). Tuck goes on to talk of punishment being a restriction of liberty, a familiar and well–rehearsed concept within the probation service. Whilst I am not suggesting that

Tuck's principles are a panacea I do think they provide a helpful framework within which to locate practice. I shall go on to make further refinements to this argument later in developing the notion of primary task. But at this point I wish to reinforce that only when the service has a clear view of what it wants and needs to deliver can steps be taken to define the appropriate management processes.

Language – the management turn-off

A major problem for the probation service, as outlined earlier, is that of management language. The language constructs, which reflect the culture of the commercial and business world, are simply a turn-off and it is easy to understand that for a workforce with humanitarian values and sociological insight to identify itself with the alien values of harsh, exploitative, competitive, commercial management, might be seen as something of a betrayal. Clearly the concepts of the business world will need adaptation if they are to fit with the culture of the probation service. But the service must make some adaptations too. Perhaps what is needed now is a conscious decision to recognise that this process has begun. As part of it, it could be legitimately expected that probation management language will be modified, developed and reshaped to meet new and changing circumstances. In doing this the use of commercial industrial management language is unavoidable as there are no other language constructs readily available. Perhaps resistance to the language reflects the resistance to the process and in the context of Mintzberg's professional bureaucracy it is understandable.

However, I would suggest that management language might be helpful to the service and provide a sense of urgency that the service has sometimes lacked. The importance of this is underlined by the apparent lack of recognition that the traditional monopoly position the probation service has had in the criminal justice system is under threat. It can no longer be taken for granted that the service will remain the sole providers of community supervision or indeed reports to courts. Mechanisms provided by the 1991 Criminal Justice Act and Organising Supervision and Punishment in the Community (Home Office, 1991) create the opportunities for fundamental changes in that competitors could emerge. Consider this possible scenario. The introduction of the 1991 Criminal Justice Act creates expectations that information will be provided for the courts quickly, in appropriate circumstances. If the probation service fails to deliver it is conceivable that courts might look elsewhere for providers of information. A similar scenario could be developed around community supervision. Whilst not seeking to be alarmist it does seem to be important that the service begins to see and respond to potential threats to its traditional role. Unease about importing new language into the services vocabulary should not mask the real issues.

Taking the initiative

The demands of the last few years, outlined in the previous chapter, have pushed the service into an almost totally reactive position and it has been difficult to look beyond the day–to–day demands. It is important, however, that the service uses its rich talents to build its own vision of the future and use the changes in the criminal justice system to exercise its influence. It is, of course, much easier to say than to achieve. With no expectation of getting it right the following is simply a contribution to the idea of the service taking the initiative. Struggling with some of the issues of values, language, the political agenda, the economic agenda, the following by John Harvey–Jones (1991) is interesting:

> First of all, don't write off the public sector, it is actually changing very fast. I meet a lot of public sector managers and I think much of the public sector is changing faster than other parts of our environment, largely because it hurts. You know, nothing changes in Britain unless there's pain. The trick is if there is too much pain it doesn't change either, so there's got to be enough pain to make it hurt.
> The people in the public sector are not a weird bunch of asteroids who've suddenly landed from outer space, they're exactly the same as the rest of us. They want to work in decent places where they've got pride in their work. There are a number of things we've done with the public sector which contribute to making it unwieldy and unmanageable. All our systems are about control and accountability, none are about necessary creativity, because we pay lousily and we have hierarchies which stretch from here to John O'Groats and back. And we try and use alleged promotions as replacements for actual money, we are grossly over–managed, grossly over–controlled, grossly under–directed. We have no vision of where we want to be or how we could be in a better world. The place is only through the goodwill of dedicated people who are actually trying to break off some of the man–made stories that have been put around them. I'm sorry about the

emotion, but I feel that they're much more sinned against than sinning (p. 19).

Whilst what Harvey–Jones says does not fit the probation service's situation precisely, much of it is applicable. Certainly the activities of the Home Office over the last few years have created the atmosphere of being over–controlled and over–managed. But as we all know in the probation service there is no growth without pain. What Harvey–Jones says which strikes chords for me is that of a vision of a better world. This cannot be a naive or sentimental concept but a vision of a potential and achievable reality. A vision for the probation service must take account of contemporary factors of the harsh realities of a changing world. It must also encompass some of the language and concepts of the business world. After all, the service is accountable to a world that is also influenced significantly by economic reality.

Developing the vision

The following is an attempt to create a vision which involves understanding the potential factors that could influence the future and consequently to conceptualise the possible position of the service within the criminal justice system.

Vision statement

1. In three years time the probation service will be recognised and acknowledged as a provider/purchaser of excellent quality programmes of supervision for offenders.

2. There will be an ongoing commitment to continually improve performance to demonstrate to our customers (the courts) that we achieve targets.

3. Our commitment to quality performance will also secure the confidence of our major stakeholders (the Home Office and the Local Authority) and consequently will ensure sufficient investment to sustain the work of the service.

4. This commitment will also secure the confidence of the community, our other major stakeholder, by informing them about the management of risk and reassuring them about the fear of crime.

5. Through partnerships with other stakeholders the service will develop its range of facilities in order to meet the

changing demands of criminal justice and family court
policy in the 1990s.

6. Our work will be underpinned by traditional service values
of care reflected in our commitment to promoting equality
of opportunity and influencing the social policy debate.

This vision statement has the service as both the provider and
purchaser of supervision programmes for offenders. Partnership is
not new and building on co–operative ventures that have already
been set up in many areas, some of which are explored in other
parts of this book, could become a method of purchasing services.
Whilst there must be a question mark about the extent to which
services will be purchased, and at this stage this can only be a
matter for speculation, other factors that might be influential are
interesting. The possible release of 'ring–fenced' money by the
Home Office for specific activities will be one way of services
securing growth and will undoubtedly lead to the voluntary sector
taking initiatives to approach services with a view to entering into
partnerships. Cash limits and future rounds of the public
expenditure surveys may ultimately produce economic hardship
and make it more difficult for local probation services to sustain
operations. As a result the purchasing of services may simply
become a cheaper option. Putting these two factors together will
leave chief officers and probation committees with some difficult
decisions to make i.e. whether to appoint staff or to purchase
packages of supervision for offenders. Whilst economies will be an
important consideration in the decision–making process a major
criterion will be the quality of the services required and on offer.
The latter is likely to become an important issue.

Excellence is something of a buzz word in industry and there
is a whole management training industry devoted to it. How will
it become important for probation? Let us look at two major areas
of service activity – court reports and offender community supervision. The numbers of offenders given community supervision
depends on a court decision and this decision is influenced by the
probation service and the confidence that it can engender
amongst sentencers. In this scenario the workload of the service is
linked to the confidence of sentencers. It follows that in attempting
to understand how confidence can be promoted feedback about
service performance becomes a key issue. Quality performance is
then equated with confidence and subsequent workload. It is a
market analogy – influencing the customers to use more of the
product. The vision statement is suggesting that performance and
the commitment to continually improving it will provide a
tangible means of convincing the courts as the customers of the

service. In order to explain the comparison it is helpful to think of the primary task of the service. I first came across the concept of primary task whilst working with the Grubb Institute on my Assistant Chief Probation Officer training in 1985. It is a useful concept of defining the core purpose of an organisation and ultimately the tasks for individuals within it. It is of course very difficult to reach agreement on any such definition and the following is proffered with diffidence and in the knowledge that it is by no means perfect. In spite of this difficulty I would argue that the concept of primary task is important, because it is a means of stating common purpose. It is a way in which an organisation can conceptualise and get in touch with its core task. An alternative way of explaining the notion is to say that it is a way of defining what an organisation is in business which could be applied to the probation service. Here is an attempt at defining primary task which has been well aired in Cleveland.

Primary task

The primary task of the probation service is to assist the courts and the criminal justice system in their decision–making and to supervise offenders in the community.

This definition covers the work of the service in all courts, including family courts, and also recognises that not all decisions about crime are made in the formal court setting. Consequently, it is an attempt to reinforce the importance of the service contribution to decision–making in all criminal justice settings. This primary task definition reflects the historical role of the service which began when Police Court Missionaries intervened in the sentencing process. The other strand of this definition, and purists of the concept might argue the most relevant one, is the supervision of offenders in the community. At present the probation service is the almost monopolistic provider of adult offender community supervision. Having reflected on the potential for change in this situation how does the service maintain its position? Beyond this and if the world does change, how does it ensure that it secures a competitive edge? First of all by recognising that the courts are its customers and that unless the sentencers are satisfied with what the service delivers they may look elsewhere.

In order for local services to deliver effectively there must be some clarity about what constitutes good quality community supervision. The courts' interpretation of what constitutes good supervision would be important too. There are, of course, other interpretations of what might constitute good supervision and national standards are already a bench mark. But often offenders have views as consumers and probation officers as professionals. However, at this stage I want to make links with the analogy of the courts as customers because they control the workload of the service through their sentencing patterns. If the service is to stay in business and maintain its resource levels then it must at least maintain or perhaps even increase its market share in high risk offenders. To achieve this result the probation service will need to know what factors in its performance influence the views of sentencers. This information should then be used to enhance performance and the results fed back to the courts.

In Cleveland The Probation '91 Event was an attempt to explore the views of sentencers. Other similar exercises have been undertaken elsewhere, but in this one questionnaires were used to gain insights into the expectations of sentencers about the work of probation officers. Some 60% of magistrates thought that the service could supervise serious offenders in the community. One magistrate gave the following view, 'probation service good concept, marvellous service, keen to see people kept out of prison. More face–to–face contact with clients needed. More of the control element needed' (Cleveland Probation Service, 1991, p.13). Such feedback may not always be comfortable but it does give some insights into expectations. These need to be heeded and translated into factors that can be recognised as components of good practice which will, in turn, satisfy the sentencers. The vision statement tries to take account of the concept of satisfying customers by recognising that only through a process of continually improving performance can the service properly expect to demonstrate its effectiveness.

Another aspect of the vision statement deals with stakeholders of the service; the groups and organisations that have an interest in the service. There are a number of stakeholders, two of whom provide service funds. The Home Office and the Local Authority might in some senses be also seen as shareholders. The advent of cash limits has left the Home Office itself as the most critical stakeholder because the financing of probation is in its hands. Certainly it would be foolish for the service to ignore the implications of this. The whole process of cash limiting and the development of national standards are clear signs that the Home Office is quite prepared to exercise its influence over service activity. As a consequence one other aspect of demonstrating effectiveness is, therefore, about keeping the Home Office satisfied. Moreover the position of Local Authorities has been changed by cash limits. Certainly their financial veto has been modified whilst their 20% contribution has remained. Whilst their financial influence may have waned somewhat, because of their political representation of the local community, their stake is still a significant one.

The concept of the community as a stakeholder is a difficult one to grapple with, but nevertheless important. The Grubb Institute (1990) articulated the importance of the community as follows:

> With the changes in local leadership in this community and the level of clarity about the basis on which it is exercised, it is difficult to determine what people really want from the criminal justice process. For opinion to be processed and represented through a national forum dilutes and distorts local concerns. There is need to express and relieve anger, but it is difficult to discover community (rather than public) opinion, as what is expressed tends to be partisan rather than corporate. This suggests attention needs to be given to the community dimension of crime (p. 7–8).

How the service begins to discharge its responsibility to its community stakeholder cannot be done in isolation from other key players in the criminal justice system, but more effort could be made in informing the community about the work of the service. However, those involved in opening probation and bail hostels will know how difficult this can be. The fear of crime and management of risk in the community should be tackled through a wider criminal justice initiative. The Grubb report suggests that

> there needs to be clear local organisation for all criminal justice agencies which can relate to all local communities; and second that the level of any specialist provision (such as probation centres) needs to be sufficiently local for communities to take some ownership of and responsibility for the provision. One of the effects of the use of imprisonment has been the avoidance of responsibility for how offenders are dealt with on behalf of local communities and society as a whole (p. 15).

There is a challenge for the service in responding to this and in developing the strategy to achieve it. What seems to emerge is the need for a coordinated criminal justice structure and some continuous process of dialogue with the community. In Cleveland a Criminal Justice Forum was set up in 1991 with a statement of purpose which meets some of these aspirations. This group comprises all the key players in the local criminal justice system: the Chairs of the Justices, the Clerks to the Justices, the Governors of prison establishments, the Chief Executive of the Local Authority, the Chief Crown Prosecutor, the Director of Social Services, the Chief Constable, the County Education Officer, the Chair of the Probation Committee, the Chief Probation Officer, and chairing the group a senior Judge. This practical initiative relates to point three of the vision statement both in terms of the confidence of the community and the fear of crime. Because the probation service cannot go it alone any more this dimension of partnership will be helpful. Finally, a restatement of probation values and of promoting equality of opportunity in a system which by nature is conservative and even reactionary seems to be an important reminder of the unique service contribution. Social policy is mentioned as a way of reinforcing that the service should have a hand in the debate and consequently an opportunity to influence.

What I think is important to reiterate is that some vision or aspiration can be helpfully articulated for the service because it is a very positive way of giving a sense of direction for the organisation as a whole. The vision will need to be amended to reflect a changing world and hopefully a growing sophistication in handling the concept. At this stage in probation history the idea of vision may seem trivial or contrived. But behind it I would argue is a useful management concept and one that may be central to the services ability to proactively influence its own future and that of the criminal justice system.

Mission – aims and values

Whilst acknowledging the language problems associated with such terminology I would also suggest that it is helpful for organisations to have a sense of mission. Historically this has not been a problem for a service deriving its existence from the pioneering work of police court missionaries. But a contemporary statement of purpose, aims and values, which is what I take the mission to be, seems a helpful part of a corporate management process. For example the language of punishment being allied to the role of the probation service in the criminal justice system needs to be tempered by humanitarian values which are part of the service's day–to–day work. The mission statement is designed to do this in a way that should be reassuring to staff. It also has something to say about the responsibilities of performance which should equally be reassuring to staff, customers and consumers. Alternative and equally relevant views about the content of this mission will be developed but a stab at a mission statement is contained in the next section.

Mission statement

The probation service's mission is to ensure the best use of community disposals within the criminal justice system. The service will seek to be a positive force in its contribution to crime prevention and community safety. In recognising the tensions that exist in society the service is committed to using its social work skills to ameliorate conflict and to promote understanding of the needs of the alienated and disaffected.

The following aims are an integral part of the service's mission and in day–to–day practice the service will:

1. Promote the dignity and integrity of the individual within the criminal justice system, the civil courts and society as a whole.

2. Challenge offending behaviour through a constantly innovative and effective range of service strategies.

3. Maintain the highest standards of practice in order to promote the confidence of courts and the community in the work of the service.

4. Meet its responsibilities to those with whom the service works – the consumers.

5. Develop effective collaboration within the community and with other agencies in order to promote effective inter–agency partnerships and to further the understanding of the role of the probation service within the criminal justice system.

6. Promote an equal opportunities strategy in all aspects of service activity.

Whilst acknowledging the inadequacies of structure and language this statement of purpose should present no problems to a committed workforce and hopefully could be a source of service identity and a dimension of corporate performance.

Staff as stakeholders

The exercise of devising vision and mission statements are a reminder of the importance of the workforce because staff are important stakeholders in the service. They are in every sense the most valuable resource accounting as they do for around 80% of the budget and are also the means by which the service is delivered and values upheld. In this management scheme it is vital, therefore, that real attention is given to articulating the crucial part that staff play in the organisation. The following corporate objective is one possible means of doing this.

Corporate staff objective

In a rapidly changing world in which the probation service will become a purchaser as well as a provider of services, the workforce will only be secured by the quality of its performance. Enhanced performance will create the need for new skills, personal growth and adaptation to meet new expectations. As part of this process staff have the right to an understanding of the objectives, tasks and targets expected of them. They equally have a right to participate in their own performance appraisal, development needs, assessment and career planning. Within the probation service this is underpinned by a commitment to staff support and quality supervision; to equality of opportunity which reinforces the importance of the contribution of each individual and ensures the proper proportionate representation of women, ethnic and other minority groups at all levels of the service.

The purpose of this statement is to convey something of the urgency created by the demanding world in which the service is now operating. Put simply, in future if better quality services can be provided more economically through partnerships and purchasing mechanisms, then the trend towards a smaller or differently constituted workforce may be irresistible. Consequently, the quality of individual performance will become more important and new skills, personal growth and adaptation to meet new expectations will be part of enhanced performance. Service managers carry the responsibility to reassure staff through these changes and spelling out expectations and a commitment to equal opportunities are part of this process. In this particular statement the idea of the proper proportionate representation of women, ethnic or other minority groups at all levels in the service may be seen as contentious. It is not meant to be so but rather a simple statement to reinforce the fact that unless these kinds of results are achieved then statements in themselves might be seen as meaningless. Service managers have to develop the strategies to ensure that objectives are turned into results.

Objectives and targets

It will be clear by now that what is being attempted is to articulate the factors that are the components of corporate performance; the essential concepts, systems and processes that give a common sense of direction and purpose to an organisation. As already acknowledged language is always a barrier to these processes and nowhere are these difficulties more acute than in the setting of objectives and targets. It is difficult to come up with anything completely new or totally incisive but what can be said is that SNOP in 1984 began to articulate a basic MBO (management by objectives) structure for the probation service. Differing defini- tions of objectives have produced a rich diversity. For example Gilpin Black, a firm of consultants has, through its effectiveness programme, promoted the concept of key output areas (KOAs) and associated objectives in many probation areas. Other models have been proffered too and out of the inevitable confusion the one area for agreement seems that an objective should be time limited and measurable. Over the last few years local services have been struggling to try to measure the achievement of their objectives. Parry-Khan (1988) reviewed objectives and their use in probation management. She saw them fuelling conflict and preferred instead the use of *ad hoc* principles which it was argued were more likely to stimulate innovation. Mintzberg (1983) explores some of the weaknesses of such a structure which were reinforced by the work of the Audit Commission (1989) which clarified the need for objectives for the probation services. However, this work did not ease the confusion about the definition of objectives and targets. Nevertheless the audit guide did go one step further, giving details of performance indicators against which the effectiveness of the service is to be measured. What emerges from this is that objectives, targets and perfor- mance indicators are all manifestations of a process designed in some way to measure the work of the service.

One of the difficulties created for the service by these develop- ments has been the notion that its effectiveness might be measured by its ability to influence courts and the sentencing process. This quite naturally has produced reservation and resis- tance, partly because it is recognised that the sentencing process is a complex one and at no stage does the service have total control over it. Whilst the courts may be influenced by the quality of court reports, other factors may take primacy when sentencing. Consequently, views are expressed that statistics and sentencing data are an uncertain measure of service performance. There are similar concerns about judging the effectiveness of the service through its ability to prevent reoffending, because there are so many factors outside the control of the supervising officer which play a part in influencing behaviour. These arguments are well–rehearsed in the probation service but we have now reached the point when the demands for efficiency and effectiveness cannot be ignored by service managers. Some measures of the way in which the service influences the courts are inevitable. A Cleveland service internal inspection report on court reports made clear links between the quality of reports and the influencing of sentencing. In other words, the quality of reports and the supervision process can influence the attitude of sentencers in taking the risk of imposing a community sentence.

Similarly, whilst the supervision process cannot be claimed to stop offending, good supervision can be a positive influence either in terms of problem-solving, practical care or support. The service should perhaps concentrate on measures that reflect the quality of supervision and devise ways in which the sentencers might be reassured by the supervision process even though not entirely successful in terms of preventing offences. We should remember that sentencers are realists who well understand the constraints probation officers experience. What I am arguing is that the probation service cannot avoid having to justify its level of resourcing through its performance. Cash limits, performance indicators and Resource Management Information Systems, are the framework to be used. It is now left to probation areas to develop their own solutions to the problem. As a contribution to the process I would suggest that an antidote to the present confusion might be through seeing probation areas operating within a broad set of objectives which give the service a general direction. These objectives would reflect the primary task, the mission and the vision statements. Expressed in this broad way these objectives could be in place for fairly lengthy periods, say three to five years. This would give the workforce and the whole operation a sense of permanence and consequently a sense of security which is necessary in a world of rapid change. Having put together this general plan, managers of area services could then begin a more detailed and specific process of target setting. These, of necessity, will have to be set in statistically measurable terms and relate to resources. Even more importantly they should be related to expectations of both the customers and stakeholders of the service. I would like to suggest that it will be helpful to have two kinds of targets, operational targets and practice targets which will now be explored in a little more detail.

The setting and achieving of operational targets will enable services to demonstrate efficiency. Efficiency and cost effectiveness will be measured in terms of resources used to create work capacity and results achieved and units will be funded at levels which equate to expectations about performance. Put simply a finite amount of money will finance a finite amount of work.

Practice targets will enable the service to demonstrate to its customers that practice is being sustained at levels which are satisfactory. Having achieved practice targets the service is then in a position to provide positive feedback to sentencers. As a consequence the sentencers should have confidence in service practice and this, in turn, should ensure that the court uses community based sentences to the maximum.

It may be helpful to look at how these targets might be developed. I will begin by using community service as an example of how operational targets might be set for a specialist unit. The starting point in this case should be to relate the target to orders. The number of orders which community service can cope with in a year must correlate to the resources available. Factors like time taken to complete orders, throughput and the average numbers of hours per order will need to be considered by managers who will have a good idea of how these should be weighted. This kind of 'intelligence' about workloads and capacities has been developed over the years, and the expertise which exists within service management units will enable the capacity of the unit to be determined in a realistic way. The operational target having been set at say 600 a year, the unit would be operating efficiently if this number of orders were received into the unit. Beyond this effectiveness would be measured by other factors such as the number of successful completions, breach rates and the quality of community work produced. In the context of the latter the culture of the unit will be important, if the offenders are sympathetically treated they will be positive and a happy workforce will be productive. The attendance figures, similarly, will be affected and if these are good the successful completion rate will be good too. Social work skills will, therefore, be as influential as ever in ensuring the effectiveness of the operation.

However, in the context of operational targets, in the above scenario if community service does not receive its 600 orders per year its efficiency will be reduced. If this falls below reasonable tolerances, in a cash limited world the resources will be under threat and will ultimately be diverted elsewhere. The problem for the community service unit is that it is able to control its own effectiveness and its secondary efficiency measures like project supervision costs, but it is not able to control the input of orders. This illustrates the interrelatedness and mutual dependency of operations within the service. As a consequence other operations have to contribute to the achievement of community service targets. This would involve court report writers and those staff representing reports in court would need to maintain an awareness of the unit's target. This might be achieved through report writers having firm operational targets of their own to ensure the achievement of the unit's target.

It would be illogical to suggest that target setting could be a precise exercise and some judgement will have to be made about how many of the high risk offenders the service could persuade the courts to place on community sentences. A close analysis of statistics would give an indication of local sentencing patterns, a sophistication already achieved in many probation areas. This information would then enable targets to be set with reasonable accuracy. For example risk of custody scores related to past local sentencing patterns would reveal the characteristics of cases in which courts might be more or less easily influenced. These judgements having been made, it might be decided that the service has a chance of influencing the courts in a proportion of cases where high risk offenders appeared before the courts. Past service performance would be a major factor to be considered here. The proportion having been decided the resulting figure would be a broad service target which would then influence the resource allocation for all the facilities the service might develop for use by the courts for high risk offenders. It would follow, therefore, that a similar exercise would need to be done for each of the other units such as, for example, day centres and hostels which are providing statutory requirements in probation orders.

I would suggest that this kind of process will be an important part of strategic thinking in future. It will be even more relevant in a cash limited situation when all operations may not be fully resourced and as a result there will be competition for funds. The basic process of operational target setting in relation to resources, I would argue, is relevant for all units. Those providing non–statutory packages and temporary release will also have to be seen as cost efficient in the future. In fact, in determining whole service priorities there will be difficult decisions to make. There will be a growing awareness of operational costs and the fact that growth in the area of work may be at the expense of another. Whilst it may not be a pleasant picture to contemplate, without the development of these new management skills it will be worse.

These issues also bring into stark relief some of the potential difficulties created by the 1991 Criminal Justice Act. Before this piece of legislation, and no doubt following it too, a number of high risk offenders were given straight probation orders, that is without any additional requirements. Operationally these orders are potentially the cheapest for the service to administer. Additional requirements add considerably to the cost of orders. It is quite possible that the attractiveness of combination orders for sentencers may in fact see these more costly alternatives preferred by courts to straight probation or straight community service orders. Such a development may not enhance the service's overall effectiveness and would in simple cost terms make it less efficient.

In beginning the process of examining the development of practice targets I would want to continue the analogy of the courts as customers. Thought will have to be given to what reassurances the customers will need in order to be satisfied that the service can effectively handle high risk offenders in the community. From personal experience of working with the Cleveland probation committee, and other sentencers from the North East and other parts of the country, standards of supervision are very important. Tangibly this includes rapid take up of the order i.e. a quick first contact followed by levels of contact which at least present the possibility of some meaningful interaction taking place between probation officer and offender. It can still be safely assumed that meaningful means helping; helping the individual avoid offending by using the values and skills that the service has developed over many years. On the face of it all this may seem straightforward, but feeding back information to sentencers about supervision results will need to be reasonably sophisticated if it is to be influential. Details of work undertaken and the impact on the offender will have to be measured in a way which offers an opportunity for the service to demonstrate the quality of work. For example, whilst it is not always possible to curtail offending behaviour it is possible to help many offenders overcome problems which contribute to their offending. The challenge is to be able to develop effective means of providing this feedback to sentencers and the achievement of targets relating to practice is one way of doing this. Setting practice targets for levels of contact is crucial because without contact there can be no influence. But other targets related to the actual process of supervision, like problem solving, will be helpful in convincing sentencers of the efficacy of supervision. If services can demonstrate that they are closely supervising offenders, doing all that they reasonably can, then sentencer confidence will be maintained. This in turn should produce community based sentences at levels which will enable the service to achieve its operational targets of numbers of orders. This is an important point because having satisfied customers and stakeholders in terms of operational performance the service will be in a stronger position to promote wider criminal justice debate about offending behaviour. Perhaps with the security of good performance the service may be able to cogently argue the links between social policy decisions and the implication for the criminal justice system.

What I am arguing, therefore, is that there are clear advantages for the probation service in setting targets which ultimately relate to values and spheres of influence. I am suggesting that targets should be set against a background of broad objectives which in themselves set a basic direction for the service. That the targets should be set on two levels, at an operational level relating to levels of resourcing which could be said to justify levels of funding and investment in the service; and also at a practice level which will enable the service to convince sentencers about the quality of the work. Perhaps even more importantly for the soul of the service I am suggesting that the achievement of both sets of targets will be a practical realisation of its values.

It is important that all staff are involved in objective and target setting. They need to understand the relevance of the process to the corporate performance of the service. Care should be taken over the consultation process which should enable staff to become aware of the demands being made on the service and the responses required in terms of performance at all levels. The process should also reassure the workforce about the importance of values in their day–to–day work.

Conclusion

This chapter has been devoted to management processes, to exploring vision and mission against a background of primary task. However, it is also important to consider the strategic issues involved in these management processes and these will be considered in the next chapter.

References

Audit Commission (1989) Probation Service Audit Guide, HMSO.

Cleveland Criminal Justice Forum (1991) Statement of Purpose.

Cleveland Probation Service (1991a) Probation '91 Event.

Cleveland Probation Service (1991b) Internal Inspection Report on SIRs.

Grubb Institute (1990) Community Crime and the Punishment of Offenders, Centre for exploration of social concerns.

Handy, C. (1985) *Understanding Organisations*, Penguin.

Harvey-Jones, J. (1991) 'Britain the troubleshooter', in *The Independent*, 22.10.91.

HM Inspectorate of Probation (1990) *Efficiency and Effectiveness Inspection in the Probation Service: The First Year*, HMSO.

Home Office (1984) *Probation Service in England and Wales: Statement of National Objectives and Priorities*, HMSO.

Home Office (1991) *Organising Supervision and Punishment in the Community*, Blue Paper Discussion Document, HMSO.

Mintzberg, H. (1983) *Structure in Fives: Designing Effective Organisations*, Prentice Hall International.

Parry-Khan, L. (1988) 'Management by objectives in probation', *Social Work Monograph*, Norwich.

Tuck, M. (1989) 'The probation service: A forward look' in R. Shaw and J. Haines (eds) *The Criminal Justice System: A Central Role for the Probation Service*, Institute of Criminology, Cambridge.

5 The strategic dimension

Roger Statham

The Statement of National Objectives and Priorities document (SNOP) of 1984 has been identified as something of a watershed in the sense that it heralded objective setting in the probation service. But in retrospect there was almost a naive expectation that the setting of objectives in themselves would lead automatically to their achievement and that as a consequence profound organisational changes would occur. An insightful observer might now ask what has really changed and proceed to conclude that real changes have yet to occur. Certainly, if change were to be measured in practice terms, that is in assessing what actually goes on between probation officer and offender, then little does seem to have changed in the context of basic interaction. It is true that over the past few years more supervision packages, involving group work, have been developed. But by and large this provision exists for only a small minority of offenders. However, the experience of the large majority of those under probation supervision remains rooted in the traditional one–to–one setting.

Having said this, factors identified in previous chapters are hastening change within the service. But how should service managers respond? The starting point has been identified in terms of recognising the importance of some essential management processes like defining primary task; having a sense of vision and mission; setting objectives and targets with both operational and practice dimensions. However, as probation areas found with objective setting in the mid–1980s, putting words on paper does not automatically make them part of corporate performance. Therefore, the translation of aspiration into performance is perhaps the ultimate management challenge in the 1990s. An essential component of this process is some over–arching strategic thinking which facilitates the achievement of goals. The concept is one of a results orientated strategy being developed through asking and answering certain key questions. Put simply, strategic thinking leads to strategic planning, leads to results.

If the gap between objective setting and achievement in the probation service is to be closed, strategic thinking and planning may be a useful bridge. It would not be helpful to be sidetracked into a lengthy debate about the origins of strategy, but to put it into perspective its roots are militaristic and as a concept it was later borrowed by business management. The adaptations have subsequently refined the thinking to the point that it could be said to accommodate the dynamics of organisations generally. The hypothesis is that it is also relevant to the probation service.

Porter (1987) identifies two strands influencing the growth of strategic planning when he says that

> The first was the developments in programme planning and budgeting that came out of the Second World War. Many companies installed formal budgeting as a tool to improve the control of their operations. Annual budgets were soon stretched into five year plans because of its growing recognition that the financial consequences of decisions were often long term.
> A second stream of thought, pioneered in the 1950s at the Harvard Business School, highlighted the importance of having an overall corporate strategy. Management theory had concentrated on the functions of business e.g. production, finance, marketing, logistics, control. Each was pursued as a separate subject, with its own concepts and methodologies. Yet there was no theory on how to integrate these functions. Companies had always had overall strategies, but these remained implicit and largely intuitive. As firms grew and became more complex, however, they needed a systematic approach to setting strategy. Strategic planning emerged as the answer.
> Strategic thinking rarely occurs spontaneously. Without formal planning systems day to day concerns tend to prevail. The future is forgotten. Formal planning provided the discipline to pause occasionally to think about strategic issues. It also offered a mechanism for communicating strategy to those who had to carry it out, something that seldom happened when the formulation of strategy remained the private province of the chief executive (p.21).

Here Porter reviews the impact of strategic thinking and planning in the business world, a world subject to fad and whim. The success of Japanese management methods brought strategy into question whilst at the same time corporate culture became a new fad as everyone went 'in search of excellence'. But he goes on to affirm the importance of strategy and that there are no substitutes for strategic thinking. Improving quality is meaningless without knowing what kind of quality is relevant in competitive terms. Nurturing corporate culture is useless unless the culture is aligned with a company's approach to competing.

Porter also goes on to put Japanese management into perspective, suggesting that whilst Japanese companies have become synonymous with quality, productivity and teamwork, they also plan. They are meticulous students of their industries and their competitors. What is also apparent is that Japanese companies have a clear view of the product and the market. Teamwork is easier to achieve in a culture in which it is natural to strive for the benefits of the whole company. In the business world there is a considerable preoccupation with organisation and culture which is underlined by the work of Handy (1985). But as Porter reminds us, one cannot ignore strategic thinking in favour of maintaining a supportive culture, just as one cannot ignore quality no matter how elegant the strategic plan (1987, p.27). He makes two other important points. Firstly that to be effective, strategic planning must use proper process, because strategy cannot be separated from implementation. Secondly, that it is not just a once a year exercise because it should inform daily activity. Strategic planning, therefore, must be part of the work of line managers and not just a headquarters unit.

It may be conceded that this kind of thinking is all very well in the business world, but how does it relate to probation management? I would argue that there are very clear parallels between business, commerce and service industries and the position of the probation service within the criminal justice system of the 1990s. For example, the Blue Paper (Home Office, 1991a) proposals in themselves have enormous implications for the management of the service. For example, how can the service be expected to deliver unless there is clear thinking about the consequences of each management component in a cash limited world? It is also important to remember again the lessons of SNOP (Home Office, 1984) in the sense that the setting of objectives does not automatically lead to their achievement. Furthermore, recent events suggest that the service's traditional monopoly is under threat and demands now being placed on the service clearly create the need for cultural shift. Perhaps some of the time traditionally devoted to philosophical debate should be now used for strategic thinking and planning in order to provide the opportunity to link together the various threads of the management process into a corporate whole.

Porter suggests that corporate strategy has two elements. One is the way the corporation adds value above and beyond what could be achieved if business units were independent. Secondly, that value can be added through the development of synergy i.e. working together (p. 28). Put simply, what is being argued is that effective cooperation within an organisation can enhance performance. This is something that is difficult to gainsay but as always the real challenge lies in achievement.

The nature of the organisation itself is a factor here. Certainly, synergy is not a concept that might be readily applied to the probation service. A loose structure based on notions of individual professionalism does not lend itself to the cohesive structure possible in some industrial settings, epitomised by Japanese organisations. Nor is it easy, or desirous, to see the probation service behaving like Johnson & Johnson, the American pharmaceuticals corporation, which uses its credo as a means of engendering the support of its workforce. The probation service needs to develop its own brand of corporate performance and style of management that suits its nature and purpose but which nevertheless allows it to change in order to meet new challenges.

Making the changes

Payne (1990) produced a useful paper in which he discussed some aspects of change in relation to work he had done with the Greater Manchester Probation Service. Payne suggests that:

> Change can only develop from a flexible and creative organisation, and the management task is to facilitate creativity, while setting the parameters and making the strategic choices which will channel change efforts most effectively. The probation service, like many fundamentally professional organisations, does not depend crucially on physical resources but on the resources of skill and know–how contained within its staff. 'Know–how' organisations need different techniques of management from those with mainly industrial and maintenance functions, and this demands special management techniques and skills which must be developed (p.1).

Payne's paper is an exploration of the theory surrounding the management of change drawing, as he does, on some important writing. He concludes by suggesting some principles for managing change:

> It is important to invest in people, and in their skills and know-how. You must empower people to act to deal with problems, by giving them the resources and offering personal involvement and effective demonstration of action by skilled managers. There must be a culture of pride in the organisation and the work, and a climate of success. Managers must encourage the development of options and not try to control too much. Crucially, however, it is management's job to take on the difficult decision, to devise strategy and be selective among the options; to avoid the responsibility for this avoids the role of management. Finally, change can be exciting, interesting and improve the service for people who need it. So we should not be frightened of it; it can be fun to take on, and it can give a feeling of achievement to succeed in implementing an effective programme of change (p.11).

These interesting conclusions raise the fundamental 'how' question. It is a tall order for managers of the probation service in the 1990s to take the responsibility for making change exciting. Other aspects, however, might be more achievable.

Whilst empowerment is explored elsewhere in this book, in the context of Payne's conclusions it seems to be about resourcing and involvement. In reviewing Payne's ideas it has to be said that resourcing and involvement are certainly not beyond an organisation which has considerable experience of people issues, consultation, and a good track record with regard to new resources. It should also be remembered that in spite of all the objective and target setting exercises, actual practice has been very much left in the hands of practitioners. So again, involvement does not seem to be a problem. Developing a climate of success is not without its difficulties considering the nature of probation work. It would not be unreasonable to suggest that the service should still take pride in the values that it brings to the criminal justice system. But perhaps the most important points that Payne develops are those concerned with management. To devise strategy and to be selective about the many options are the difficult decision that managers cannot avoid. Clearly, there are potential tensions between the concept of empowerment, not controlling too much, and making decisions. These particular tensions are reflected in the very nature of the probation service as an organisation. As articulated earlier, with a lack of workforce consensus about either primary task or the role and functions of the probation service; a strong culture of 'professional independence' (autonomy);

empowerment is a difficult concept. It might be easier to make progress in this area as the service develops clarity of purpose and so the 1991 Criminal Justice Act might yet be a golden opportunity.

Perhaps the crucial factor is that of positive perception. In the probation service it has become too easy to see the negatives in everything. It can be more difficult to see the positives for as Wasik and Taylor (1991) stated:

> Probation Officers expressed disquiet in respect of the impending changes to the rationale, structure and organisation of the probation service. This echoed the service's opposition to many of the changes proposed in the Green Paper, Punishment and Supervision in the Community, issued by the Home Office in February 1990. They commented that the proposals in the Bill would 'further reduce morale in a service already demoralised by government proposals to toughen community penalties by such means as introducing curfews' (p. 6).

It would be a pity if legitimate concerns about electronic tagging and curfews clouded the potentially positive aspects of the new legislation.

It will be important for the probation service not to see the Act as constraining or to see national standards as a paradigm against which there can be no local variation. The important point about national standards is that they become a guarantee of baseline practice on which much more can be built. The standards in themselves do not take away the opportunity for innovation which should still be part of the practice aspiration of each individual probation officer. The structure of standards in itself surely should not inhibit performance, especially when it is remembered that over the years there have been a number of mechanisms of accountability (Home Office inspection and case committees being examples). In their era these were complied with purposefully as national standards should be. It is simply not credible to argue that the structure provided by national standards denies space to innovate.

On the other hand it would have to be conceded that lack of resources might. If resources are to be secured through performance then the 1991 Criminal Justice Act with its new philosophy of proportionality and protection may provide an opportunity. The Act seems to provide an opportunity to move away from so–called deterrents and to make community options the major plank of sentencing. There is also an intention to ensure that previous offending records do not play an overly negative part in sentencing. Although there are some criticisms of the new legislation because of the links with notions of punishment in the community, its structure should not inhibit the work of a skilled and committed workforce, particularly when there is very little that is new, except perhaps an expectation of positive action to engage with offenders.

What I am attempting to argue here is that even when there may be a negative perception of national standards and punishment in the community, there is an equally valid alternative view. Promoting the alternative view, when there are also feelings about being over–managed following the national standards initiatives, will not be easy. The challenge to managers to create a climate in which change seems exciting and interesting is a considerable one. Perhaps this process might begin by offering some reassurance to the work force; reassurance that the basic values of the service still hold good and will not be lost. That some of the basics the service does well will provide a decent foundation on which to build for the future. For example, practice development has always been, and will remain, the collective aspiration of the service. Good supervision in which coaching and support extend the capacities of the individual will still be the cornerstone of performance. Whilst the number of training courses may diminish, commitment to individual development will remain high. Equally, the focus may change as recognition grows that what is needed is a learning culture in which individual commitment to personal practice development is underpinned by a proper appraisal system, using as many objective criteria as possible. The impending changes will also provide the opportunity for proper task definition and expectations of every post holder being clearly spelled out. As a result, staff will need to learn about the components of corporate performance; the purpose of the organisation; its general direction, aims, objectives and targets informed by practice guidelines; performance measured through monitoring, inspection and appraisal. The key to this seems to be in each individual member of the workforce being able to perceive their own unique contribution to the whole. In order to move to this position, some important decisions and actions need to be taken by senior managers.

Towards a strategy

Welding the probation service into a series of cohesive local organisations is no easy task but nor is it impossible. A pre-requisite is the determination of chief officers and their committees grasping the nettle of creating their vision of the future, developing associated objectives and targets, and a strategy for delivering them. Strategic thinking will be an important and ongoing process which should be results orientated. It should also be accompanied with a determination to make progress. Put simply, it is the start of a management process of making something happen. But this in itself poses some basic questions about management style which can be illustrated by differentiating between managers and bureaucrats: managers ensure that systems produce and make things happen, whilst bureaucrats are merely content with systems maintenance. The importance of the concept that managers move things on lies in the fact that it ultimately affects the way in which managers think and perform. When planning a journey decisions need to be taken about modes of transport, times of departure, times of arrival, how the systems coordinate. It is not simply a question of jumping on any old train expecting to arrive. Furthermore, a fall–back strategy is needed if the train is missed or late. This simple illustration demonstrates the complexity of the processes involved. Successful journeys are usually made successfully because individuals have developed sufficient expertise.

The same facility, strategic thinking, is needed in order to achieve any management task. The route to the achievement of objectives and targets needs to be carefully planned and some thought should be given to what might go wrong. Pulling together some disparate threads and drawing upon learning at the Henley Management College, I have attempted to fashion some questions which might lend themselves to probation management strategic thinking. They are simply a starting point and could no doubt be considerably improved upon.

1. What results are you trying to achieve?

2. Have you control over all the processes involved?

3. Do you have the authority needed to accomplish the task?

4. Whose/what support do you need in order to deliver?

5. How are you going to secure them?

6. What are the potential risks you are trying to avoid?

7. What are the resource implications?

8. Do you need a fall-back position?

Having posed the questions let us examine each of them in a little detail.

1.   What results are you trying to achieve?

Perhaps one of the most difficult aspects of change for the probation service is that it will have to become more of a results organisation. Some might prefer outcomes to results, and the difference may be semantic, but results seem more definite. It seems to suggest that effort and activity are designed to achieve a particular end and management strategy, I would argue, is about just that. It is not simply about travelling hopefully, although at times we all may have to settle for that, but it is about being clear about the results we want to achieve. At the beginning of any management process it is important to know what results are required. For example, a manager in a specialist unit will need to know the number of orders required in a year. The unit will be resourced to that level and failure to achieve the target will jeopardise resources. Similarly, if planning a public relations strategy it is important to know what results are expected. It provides the means of measuring effort against performance; the justification of the resources; the quality of the work. This basic question can be applied to something as complex as setting whole service targets or a team meeting. It could be said that activity without result has no purpose and it can also be an expensive waste of resources.

2.   Have you control over all the processes involved?

This begins the process of focusing on strategy and recognising that there will be a whole series of events before the result is achieved. If the events are all within the compass of one individual they may be easily achieved. But often processes involve other players who may have different perceptions and/or methods of working. There will be a need for mutual clarity to be developed if individuals are to work towards the same ends. The posing of this question opens up the degree of complexity of the task being undertaken. The time taken to think this through will be a key factor in achieving a successful result.

3.   Do you have the authority needed to accomplish the task?

An important question at any level in the organisation. Having the authority usually means that the resources will be available and that there will be no blocks put in the way by colleagues or superiors. For example, it may be proper for a manager to want to reorganise civil work, but in order for this reorganisation to be successful the support, approval and permission of many individuals will be needed. There are many examples even in a supportive culture like the probation service of project work being begun only to founder because it is sabotaged by colleagues. It is better to have the authority to amend in the first place by ensuring that firm proposals or terms of reference for feasibility work are agreed. The alternative might be a good deal of wasted effort.

4. Whose/what support do you need in order to deliver?

This complements the third question. It may be that there has to be a constant process of checking out the strategy with key players to ensure that resistance is not suddenly placed in the way of results being achieved. The support needed may be of individuals or organisations. It will be important to think this through in order to know the structure and workings of the organisation if an internal project is being considered, or other organisations and networks if external.

5. How are you going to secure them?

Having identified the supports needed in order for the result to be achieved it is essential to obtain them. If a partnership is being developed, funding may be as crucial as the support of key players. In the case of individuals it may be the challenge of winning hearts and minds. The tactics used will vary; consultation, hard bargaining and even direction, will all be necessary in appropriate situations.

6. What are the potential risks you are trying to avoid?

In a service which believes that it takes a positive view of most things, this may seem like a strange question. It is included here simply to reinforce the fact that neither processes nor individuals should be taken for granted. Even in the probation service there are those who might wish to scupper what the organisation is trying to achieve. But more often there are problems because the potential risks simply have not been anticipated or thought through. Having done this, it is essential to develop a scheme to avoid or ameliorate them. Tactics will have to be devised to suit each situation.

7. What are the resource implications?

On the face of it this is perhaps the simplest question. However, it needs to be answered thoroughly, which includes an appreciation of both the medium and long term dimensions. The arrival of cash limits has made this the most crucial question and it is one that is likely to precipitate most change to management culture. The questions will become almost a reflex response to any future project, because ultimately new tasks might well only be developed at the expense of current operations. A simple example would be the extra resources needed to meet the likely demand for combination orders so that extra capacity in day centres and community service might only be provided if parallel savings are made elsewhere in the overall operation. If resource levels are good then this may not be a problem, but it is difficult to envisage that the service will avoid some financial constraints after cash limits have been introduced.

8.   Do you need a fall-back position?

The answer generally might well be 'yes' because contingency planning will inevitably be needed. It is surely too simplistic to believe that in spite of strategic thinking and planning the results will always be achieved. Some compromise may be needed along the way. It will be helpful to have given this some thought at the beginning of the process. However, it is also important to recognise that some results may be absolutely paramount if resource levels are to be maintained. For example, a community service unit may have to reach its targets in order to sustain a given level of resourcing. In simple terms, if the results are not delivered then the resource levels will not be able to be maintained in that unit. The 'excess' will be used elsewhere, perhaps to respond to unmet need elsewhere. A further example of a fall-back position would be in a situation in which some operational change is planned to be implemented by a given date; factors may emerge that necessitate change which simply could not have been anticipated at the planning stage. Perhaps it is worth adding the rider that care should be taken not to move to a fall-back position which undermines the eventual achievement of the result.

There is an important point to reinforce about the use of these or any other strategic questions; that is creating the space to ensure that they are fully explored. Reactive management is unavoidable in a demanding day–to–day world but real thought does need to be given to key issues. This will require time and strategic questions need to be explored fully if they are to be effective. An exercise half done will not ensure the achievement of results and will simply be wasted effort.

Answering these questions fully should create the framework

of a strategic plan which in turn should ensure that the results are delivered. Issues like the attitudes of staff, resources, training, consultation, information, monitoring and review, should all emerge from the process. These questions are not proffered as a panacea but as a contribution to moving towards a culture that is results orientated. The holding of meetings or the setting of an objective is not all that the management process requires. I would suggest that strategy is the essential mortar between the bricks of objectives and targets, and the structure of probation management which delivers results. There can be no pretence that these skills will be developed easily but the task of developing a management culture relevant to the probation service is timely.

Having begun strategic thinking and planning it has to be recognised that the probation service is not suddenly going to become a results orientated organisation. The probation service has a totally different culture and history to that of commercial organisations and consequently the starting point for change is different. It will be important to preserve the best of the present, the innovation, commitment and values. But as change is inevitable, what kind of organisation will the service become? We may answer that it is one which holds on to the best of the past but looks to the future. Cultural change, it could be argued, should come from a reorientated senior management which itself recognises the new agenda for the service and is prepared to rise to the challenge. Inevitably, this will demand structural and operational modifications too, but the major issue is one of leadership.

Leadership in management

Statham (1990) has already reviewed the changing demands for the various echelons of service management and it can safely be said that management is still in transition. Chief probation officers in both shire and metropolitan areas are becoming more and more like managing directors who head growing and increasingly complex operations.

The leadership role exemplified by Lile (1986, p. 78) not only carries within it the responsibility for strategic thinking and planning, but for systems and people management. The rapidity of change for those at the top of the probation organisation has been gruelling; change has been greater here than anywhere else in the organisation. But demands will not lessen and as the full impact of Resource Management Information System (RMIS) and cash limits are felt it is likely that the discomfort will grow. Whilst chief officers strive to maintain links between service values and operations, financial and economic considerations will inevitably assume even greater operational import.

Within local services, operational changes will be necessary to ensure appropriate levels of expertise within headquarters units. The steps taken by the ex–metropolitan areas in employing their own secretaries and treasurers are ultimately likely to be necessary in the shires too. Whilst the precise route and thinking is not yet clear, it does seem apparent that local authorities are unlikely to be able to deliver effective services to probation areas without some major modification. For example, local probation services are likely to become formal customers of local authorities with service level agreements being tight financial contracts. Economics will play an increasing part in determining how services manage practice and also operations like finance, personnel and information systems. Ultimately, I would argue that there will be such a need for operational sophistication that finance, personnel and information systems will be necessary in–house. It will then be just a short step to having free standing shire counties and the boundary commission review may hasten this in some cases.

But the real tension for chief probation officers is likely to be through the linking of performance to resources. National standards and performance indicators are likely to be used as criteria for funding in future. As a consequence, systems will need to be in place which will ensure that quality performance is consistently delivered. This in turn will focus attention on middle manager performance because it will be they who have the responsibility of ensuring service delivery and in this context they are key players. Leadership will be a part of the task of each manager in the service.

The art of delegation will achieve a greater significance and meaning, and deputy chief probation officers, assistant chief probation officers, secretaries, treasurers, finance managers, personnel managers, information managers, administrative officers *et al*, will all play significant roles. But reflecting the views of Harvey–Jones (1982) the orchestration will be in the hands of the chief. Therefore, the effectiveness of systems, the performance of subordinates, links with the outside world, advising the probation committee and leading the service, are all parts of leadership. This is a demanding role to say the least and it is interesting that during a period of major evolutionary change within the service, there has been little or no formal training for chief probation officers. The formal induction consists of two days in the Home Office, although there has been some commitment to sponsoring places on other more formal management courses for the fortunate few. Change in management training is overdue and there now needs to be a real attempt to develop a curriculum that is probation specific.

There are corollaries for all managers in the probation service in the above. What emerges is that leadership will demand that chief officers grapple with providing some of the answers. The discomfort of this should be offset by remembering that one aspect of leadership, managing people, is a particular skill within the probation service. Furthermore, there are already signs of growing management sophistication, but in a climate of rapidly imposed change yet more management skills will have to be developed. Where is the initiative for this development coming from? The Home Office has been the traditional coordinator of management training but it has to be said that provision has been patchy and must surely be improved. Handling as many issues as they do, how can the service be sure that the Home Office will deliver? Is there a role here for the Association of Chief Officers of Probation (ACOP)?

ACOP

1991 was a year of considerable change for this senior managers' association in probation. Having committed itself to a structural review a good deal of energy was expended in constitutional amendments and restructuring at its annual conference in 1992. These changes can be said to have mirrored shifts in the probation service generally but change is not yet complete. In this context it is interesting to speculate further.

The ACOP structure places great demands on chief officer grade in the service because the work of the Association expects much in terms of time and energy. For chief probation officers in particular there are enormous tensions in the competing demands of their paid posts and offices within the Association. It speaks much of the personal commitment of all chief officer grades that so much is achieved both through ACOP and in terms of managing local services. It could be argued that the major value of ACOP lies in its interface with the Home Office and in the 1990s it can truly be said to have come of age in this respect. On short deadlines with issues of complexity like national standards and legislation, ACOP's sane and steady influence has been brought to bear. This has been clearly exemplified on the issue of cash limits. The work of the resource planning group in particular has been a major factor in ensuring reasonable resource levels for the service in its first cash limited year. No great claims need be made for this success, for everyone in the service knows that probation would have been more poorly resourced had it not been for this work. Through this ACOP demonstrated that it could coordinate fast lane information that could be persuasive at the highest levels in the government machine. Through this single exercise ACOP seems to have justified and ensured its existence.

But what of its future contribution? At this point it is appropriate to return to the issue of training. In spite of the focus and thrust provided by Training Scrutinies (Home Office, 1991b) the slow implementation of the proposals suggests a lack of enthusiasm within the Home Office. As a result the issue of management training remains unsatisfactory in the context of present need. One way forward might be for ACOP to take responsibility for organising and delivering management training. Certainly, enough expertise exists within the Association for it to be able to assess the kind of management training required. Beyond this it would simply be a question of securing the trainers on a contract basis using funding obtained from the Home Office. Potentially, there are considerable infrastructural savings to be made and the Home Office would have the safeguard of withdrawing funding if arrangements did not meet their criteria.

This kind of innovative development would help reinforce ACOP's role as the pre–eminent probation management organisation. It would also be a step towards creating a management ethos reflecting probation's unique culture. This itself is one of the major challenges of the 1990s. Position statements are fine as far as they go but the real management agenda is the strategic one. The enhancement of management performance within each of the local probation areas is an essential part of an effective service performance within the criminal justice system. ACOP has now to make this leap, essentially through seeing itself as a management organisation that is also promoting the work and values of an agency within the criminal justice system. If this means enhancing and expanding the secretariat function of ACOP, so be it. Greater capacity here would facilitate faster responses to national issues and enhance the development of management culture. In turn this would enable the service to counteract the centralist tendencies of the Home Office on the one hand and the threat of the independent sector on the other.

One area in which the service will need to develop greater expertise is in the area of financial management. It is difficult to envisage all the changes that will flow from cash limits but the financial dimension will be the primary consideration in practically every decision. Probation managers will be working in a new climate where every cost consideration will be paramount and financial management will be the primary feature of new learning. Middle managers will have a key role to play here for it will be they who have the day–to–day operational decisions to make which affect staff. It will be the middle managers who experience resistance and reaction from the workforce. It is important, therefore, that middle managers do not feel isolated and they need to see themselves as an integral part of the management group.

A social policy strategy

Whilst concentrating heavily on the development of a probation management culture I want to argue that there is also a responsibility for the service to take a wider view of its position in the criminal justice system; wide enough to consider its role in social policy matters. It has been stated that:

> The focus of central government's current intervention in relation to Criminal Justice is to try to reduce the use of custody and to reduce offending. As far as social provision is concerned, for example in relation to housing, employment and social security, the approach of central government is intended to promote people's independence and choice. If successful both approaches may lead to the deprived and marginalised becoming more confident and self–reliant. However, they may result in a greater degree of social control being imposed on an ever increasing section of the population who do not conform to expectations.
>
> The Criminal Justice process needs to strike a delicate balance: to limit the application of criminal law and the extent of social control so that it promotes responsibility and discipline among young people without undermining their capacity and confidence. This emphasises the need to value the person who offends, but the criminal justice process has failed to do this (Grubb Institute, 1990, p.3).

Some important points are raised by this article which goes on to explore a community reaction to crime as an alternative to the centralist national approach currently being pursued. As always, it is difficult to define community but we are reminded that there is a gap between criminal justice agencies and local communities. In responding to national initiatives the probation service must remember that there is little understanding of crime in the community. Furthermore, as the fear of crime grows through media coverage the probation service may have to explain its own role and functioning if communities are to be reassured by the service's ability to manage risk. Perhaps the service does have some responsibility to enable the community to take some responsibility for the ownership of offenders and for the provision of measures to supervise them. Such a dialogue would also open up aspects related to the issue of social control.

Another dimension to this particular set of issues is added by seeing offenders as victims of crime (Association of Chief Officers of Probation, 1992), which examines the lifestyles of a number of offenders. This reveals disturbing pictures of alienation, victimisation and a sense of injustice and provides a reminder that criminal justice and social policy are inextricably linked. It might seem almost naive to suggest that they are somehow not linked, but there are clear indications that criminal justice is operated with a focus on individual behaviour that largely ignores social and environmental factors in the lives of offenders. It could be argued that this situation prevails because of the lack of an effective lobby presenting alternative evidence about the effects of social policy decisions. A legitimate part of any future probation management strategy should surely include the development of an effective social policy lobby because the links between criminal justice and social policy are factors in the work of probation staff. If poverty, unemployment and poor accommodation are all factors in the lives of offenders, how can the problems be addressed? Perhaps through the development of local service strategies which should ensure that the problems are measured and ameliorated as far as practicable in the context of each individual case. At the same time local information should be used to influence the lobby strategy which might also be extended to equal opportunities.

What are the issues for probation practice? The management challenge lies in recognising that without some coordinated approach to these issues they are likely to be subjects for exchanges of rhetoric. Therefore what I am arguing is that the probation service is uniquely placed to bring influence to bear on government processes. Citizenship qualifies everyone for equality of opportunity and fairness. It would be sublime to think that in reality it could be easily achieved. Nevertheless improvements in welfare and criminal justice systems might be facilitated by a probation management structure better resourced and organised so that it was more able to draw together and articulate all intelligence at its disposal. This is simply another example of the wide application of strategic thinking.

Conclusion

This chapter has attempted to open up some of the wider

management issues in probation and to bring them together in the context of the strategic dimension. Beginning with an examination of culture and the implications of corporate performance, the management of change has emerged as an important dimension. Within this the leadership roles of managers have been seen as important. There could be no claim that all of these issues have been dealt with fully; they have been subordinated to some extent to the central themes of strategic thinking and planning. The emerging proposition is that the acquisition of strategic thinking and planning skills seem to be important for a service which is increasingly being held to account for its performance. The development of a culture in which results become a legitimate focus seems to be a sensible management response to new demands. Strategic questions have been developed with this in mind which are proffered simply as a starting point. It is recognised that these questions may need much modification before they truly inform management processes in probation. However, the importance of strategic thinking and planning would seem to be an essential part of management and it is being suggested that they deserve a high priority.

Strategic thinking and a results orientation will in themselves contribute to the agendas of change for the service. In an ideal world it may be possible for the managers and workforce to come together in some common understanding of issues and their implications. Perhaps because of the nature of the probation service and the rapidity of change to which it has been subjected, this will not be readily achievable. Constant change increases organisational tension, which in turn creates the need for clear leadership. The translation of leadership in probation has clear implications for chief officers, other senior managers and middle managers. Furthermore, ACOP should increasingly see itself as the probation management organisation. By enhancing its skills and resources it is well placed to give a lead on all management matters and a high ACOP profile might reassure the Home Office about the management and work of the service which may help temper the government's more centralist tendencies. Consequently, local differences might come to be seen as legitimate variations against a background of secure quality performance.

Within this shift towards strategic thinking and to more effective management there is a place for influencing government thinking with regard to both criminal justice and social policy issues. If there are national agendas there are local ones too in helping communities understand more about the nature of crime and the work of the service. These too would be achieved within the strategic dimension. Finally, this chapter has been an attempt to put down a series of markers which need a response, examination and modification. I hope my thoughts will be seen as a contribution to the development of a unique probation service management culture, which is essential in the 1990s.

References

Association of Chief Officers of Probation (1992) *A Sense of Justice: Offenders as Victims*, Lancaster University.
Grubb Institute (1990) Crime and the Punishment of Offenders.
Handy, C. (1985) *Understanding Organisations*, Penguin.
Harvey-Jones, J. (1982) *Making It Happen*, Collins.
Home Office (1984) *Probation Service in England and Wales: Statement of National Objectives and Priorities*, HMSO.
Home Office (1991a) Organising Supervision and Punishment in the Community: A Decision Document.
Home Office (1991b) Report of a Scrutiny of Probation in Service Training.
Lile, E. A. (1986) Corporate Leadership in Theory and Practice, *Journal of General Management*, Vol. 12.
Payne, M. (1990) The Creative Management of Change, Manchester Polytechnic.
Porter, M. (1987) Corporate Strategy, *The Economist*, 23.5.87.
Statham, R. S. (1990) *Probation in the Market Driven World*, Cleveland Probation Service.
Wasik, M. and Taylor, R.D. (1991) *Blackstone's Guide to the Criminal Justice Act 1991*, Blackstone Press.

6 Management and empowerment: the paradox of professional practice

Brian Fellowes

The purpose of this chapter is to explore the tensions which exist between practice and the management of practice in the context of broad service concerns. It is suggested that these tensions are a necessary prerequisite for the healthy development of a coherent and competent organisation working in a tough personal social service environment. If recognised and used wisely, (that is with an awareness of their positive value) they can help to ensure that the service continues to develop both its practice and its management performance effectively. Effectively, that is in terms of the service's contribution to the functioning of the criminal justice system and to the reduction of re–offending.

At the time of writing some of the more extreme ideas about how the service might have operated seem to have disappeared. The service is embarking on changes in funding arrangements; introducing the different financial requirements of Home Office cash limits (not new, of course, just different from Local Authority cash limits). In gearing up to introduce the Children Act and the Criminal Justice Act the service is rightly being required to give account for its performance, but not, it seems, required to change its orientation totally. The full implications of this new reality are still to be properly worked through (Audit Commission, 1991). Perhaps it is sufficient to say at this stage that whilst some satisfaction can be gained from the way in which the service has weathered the storms of recent years, complacency would be inappropriate as there is much more change to come. Indeed it is important that, rather than wait for change to be foisted upon it, the service's managers take advantage of the opportunities afforded by anticipating and planning for change, especially in the field of equal opportunities, training and practice development. Political imperatives may now be less pressing, but the changes wrought by technology, by changing patterns of work, by changes in training as well as by the changing social, economic and public opinion environment in which the criminal justice system operates, all these and more will press their demands on all aspects of the service. By seeing these changes as opportunities rather than threats, and by seeking to take the initiative in dealing with appropriate community crime concerns, new models can be found in both practice and the management of practice. Such developments can enhance the service's capacity to fulfil not only its primary task of reducing reoffending but also its potential for leadership in the development of health community attitudes towards crime and crime reduction. In exploring the issues concerning the tension between management and practice it is as well to contemplate the emergence of a service geared to a permanent dynamic for change rather than to a form of self–deluded stability in which more and more energy is absorbed in trying to keep things as they are.

It could be said that the events of the last few years have marked the transition from a small vocational service paddling its own rather precious canoe to a major supplier of information and expertise about crime and offenders working in partnership with other agencies within the criminal justice system. The tensions to be examined are signified not least by the shift from a service delivered by individual probation officers working relatively inde-pendently to one which employs the skills of a range of staff from a number of disciplines, who work in teams to undertake a variety of tasks, of which but one is the application of social work methods to the amelioration of criminal behaviour (Haxby, 1978).

If the service is to fulfil its potential as a force for positive change playing a central role within the criminal justice system, it must demonstrate that the tension between practice and management can be used creatively to fashion new approaches to the service's work, rather than permitting the tensions to remain at the level of a self–limiting and debilitating internal wrangle.

In order to ensure this it is necessary for managers to accept and appreciate the creative possibilities of cultural diversity and the expression of different shades of opinion in the service. The service has sometimes appeared to take a rather perverse pride in the recruitment of highly individualistic people. Many of course, are talented and often gifted practitioners, who bring to the service a rich variety of experience. The outspoken expression of opinion and genuine differences in attitude has always been a feature of the service. These differences have occasionally spilled over into the public domain to the embarrassment and sometimes dismay of the service's supporters. Tolerance, indeed encouragement of the expression of which differences is important in a service which depends on the skill, creativity and ingenuity of its practitioners. It is through such processes of debate and struggle that new ideas to cope with familiar problems and the generation of ways of handling new problems can be found. This in turn demands a high level of skill in managers in both the setting of the framework within which ideas can be heard and tolerated, and also the sense of purpose which harnesses the energy of all staff to achieve the service's aims. These very differences and variations of opinion can, of course, be used to resist change. It is important though, to see resistance to change as a step in the change process, rather than evidence of a stifling and bloody–minded conservatism. Notwithstanding the loudly articulated and trenchant expression of opposition to every change ever proposed, especially from government, the service has demonstrated a flexibility and resilience as well as creativity in absorbing and responding to the many changes presented. The resistance has in itself been important not least because it has challenged those who have sought to implement change to be clear about the grounds for which change has been regarded as necessary. The public nature of this resistance which shocks so many people outside the service has often appeared counter–productive to a service with aspirations for self–confidence and belief in its work. Close examination will reveal however, that whilst resistance has been expressed, often by particular minorities in the service, change has nonetheless occurred.

A good example of the process at work followed the introduction of the Tackling Offending Initiative introduced by the Home Office in 1988 (Home Office, 1988). This was a powerful attempt by the Home Office to 'encourage' the service to concentrate its efforts on 17 to 21 year old offenders, on the basis that successes in reducing the flow of juveniles through the criminal justice system could be extended to the higher age group. (The thinking underpinning the initiative has clearly influenced the design of measures being introduced by the Criminal Justice Act 1991.) The response of the service was far from enthusiastic, mainly because the initiative appeared to cut across a good deal of what was already happening in individual services. The movements sought by the Home Office did nevertheless take place. There was a sharp refocussing in the service's response to young offenders although many in the service would probably deny any suggestion that the changes had anything to do with the Home Office's initiative.

There is an important point to be made here about the nature and precision with which changes are required of the service especially by the Home Office. It is conceded that under some circumstances very precise and detailed requirements must be set down which brook no argument from the service. An example would be the introduction of the new Combined Order (allowing courts to sentence offenders to a single order containing elements of both community service and probation supervision) envisaged in the Criminal Justice Act. This change is ultimately to be seen as the exertion of the sovereign will of Parliament. The Act may be very specific in its requirements of the service. There are many other areas, though, where function of the Home Office must be to point the way in general terms and leave the due process of management and committee operation to take the service towards the objective in its own inimitable way. This requires some forbearance on the part of officials and a clear distinction has to be made between asserting the accountability of the Home Office to ensure that Parliament's will is done without falling into the trap of usurping the role of managers by seeming to manage the service itself. Essentially this process should be seen as an empowering process whereby the general framework within which government wishes the service's work to be pursued is established, leaving committees and managers with the space and the authority to carry out their functions. The current work to identify a national Statement of Purpose will be fine as long as area services will not be required to adopt a carbon copy without adaptation to suit local circumstances. This need for local area adaptation is vital if the service is to achieve a sense of ownership for change, rather than a knee–jerk response which might look alright on the surface but will change little in practice.

There appears to be no reason to lack confidence in the service's future as long as the tensions between practice and management and between the Home Office and area service's are understood and used creatively. The primary source of this tension lies in the nature of the twin disciplines of management and practice. The overlap between those skills required to practice successfully in social work and those required to practice successfully as a manager have long since been recognised. The two approaches speak from essentially the same body of theory. What differentiates the world of practice from the world of management is more a question of standpoint than fundamental disagreement over the body of theory and knowledge of people and how they operate in their relations with others and the wider community.

It is the case, nonetheless, that there is a continuing tension over the exercise of managerial authority in relation to practice. Indeed it is tempting to suggest, at the risk of incurring wrath from both sides of the debate, that the fact of this tension is in itself an indicator of the close relationship between the disciplines of practice and that of management. Signs of this tension have included:

- the long and apparently difficult period of transition in the role of senior probation officer from that of the first-among-equals-casework-consultant to that of team manager (Haxby, 1978, p.4)

- the persistent if forlorn yearning in some parts of the service for the 'leaderless team', which was a popular motion at NAPO conferences during the 1970s and early 1980s

- the strength of the resistance to the idea of corporate and organisational accountability

- the totemic clinging to 'professional autonomy' as a defence against the perceived onset of 'managerialism' (Haxby, 1978, p.6)

It has to be said in defence of those who have argued that the development of managerial practices is somehow wrong for the probation service, that the exercise of any competence in managerial skills within the service is a fairly recent phenomenon. The standard of managerial performance whilst not uniformly poor in former years, left a lot to be desired. The change from the idea that the service was there to be 'administered', to the notion that the work of the service should be 'managed', left many in the senior and chief officer grades (significantly then called Principal Probation Officers) increasingly adrift and bemused. Social work in a former age had taught them to care, right enough, but it had not taught them how to handle industrial relations. As services grew in size and complexity in the 1960s and 1970s, the muddles resulting from lack of attention by many retiring senior staff to the basic necessities of collective or organisational health such as policy formulation and budgeting, left their successors with much to sort out. Many of the early administrators were caring in their approach to staff and were much respected for their commitment to the values of the service and their assiduity in promoting them, but not for their managerial skills.

There has been a great change over the last few years and, driven at least in part, by a workforce noted for its inability to suffer fools gladly, the learning curve for those in managerial positions has been quite steep. It is important in this debate though, to remember that there has been little history and tradition of management in the service and that even the most rudimentary management training for chief officers is no more than a couple of decades old. Indeed, even now management training of senior and chief officer grades has rightly been criticised for its limited resources and its lack of coherence.

The contention is not that the body of knowledge which social workers and managers share leads necessarily to tension and difficulty, only that because of the overlap in theory and practice a shift in standpoint which is crucial to understanding and effective practice in both management and social work fields is necessary. Effective social workers are inclined to make good managers only to the extent that they can assimilate that crucial shift in standpoint.

Well, what is this shift about and why should it be the case that not all effective social workers become effective managers? This question requires an examination of the nature of practice and of the managerial task and some teasing out of the differences. Although the discussion concentrates on the service's work with the supervision of offenders it is acknowledged that the same fundamental issues are present in other areas of its work. Whatever else the service may be about, in the supervision of offenders, changing behaviour in order to reduce offending must be a primary goal. By definition, the offending behaviour represents a disjunction with, and an antithesis to, law abiding behaviour; a discontinuity with socially acceptable ways of behaving, however brief and temporary.

The service's task is to do whatever is possible within the contemporary moral and philosophical climate to change client's patterns of thought and action and to encourage socially acceptable and crime free responses, even if this means challenging the culture which allows crime to be deemed 'normal'. In order to do this staff exercise their skills, knowledge and ability to engage with the offender. By establishing trust, assessing the offender in the context of his/her social situation and creating a plan of work with which the client agrees and carrying it through, the worker seeks to neutralise the forces apparent in the offender's life which elicit a criminal response and encourages and reinforces those elements which will discourage crime. For the most part the task will include challenging patterns of thinking about crime, replacing poor self image with a better one, providing positive affirmation whenever possible for steps the offender takes to grasp control of, and accept responsibility for, his or her own actions. It will also include clearly articulating the costs and sanctions to the offender and potential victims of continuing criminal activity and holding the offender to account for his or her contractual obligations under the terms of an order. This approach whether used as part of a probation day centre package, or in a group setting, or in the context of routine interviews or home visits is both surprisingly effective and difficult to undertake and sustain in the face of massive and deeply rooted chaos.

It is about working *with* offenders, rather than *on* them, facing them with the consequences, both positive and negative of their behaviour, and persuading them to appreciate that the benefits of a crime free response to the pressures of life is both possible and desirable. Essentially it is about empowering the offender to find ways of being which do not prey on others' weaknesses, or repeat past mistakes and failures. It is not about haranguing, oppressing, creating dependence or providing false reassurance or setting unreal expectations. Of course it does not always work, because the forces marshalled to encourage a criminal response may simply be too overwhelming or entrenched to be overcome. There is, though increasing support for such approaches, which rightly consign the depressing 'nothing works' school of criminological and penal thought to the archival dustbin where it belongs. It appears that these methods are especially effective when staff:

- are well motivated

- are prepared to challenge patterns of thought which depersonalise victims

- tailor their work as precisely as possible to the individual needs of the offender

- are able to convey enthusiasm and optimism in their dealings with offenders and important figures in their lives (Ross, 1990, p.8).

In order to empower offenders in this way it is necessary for staff to feel confident in the exercise of their skills, to entertain a proper humility in their approach to their own skill development and a determination to find ever more effective ways of working from their own experience and that of their colleagues. They need to know that their service is both valuing and closely supporting their work as well as holding them to account and challenging them to develop their skills. They need to appreciate that their efforts with their clients form part of a wider and deeper effort by all their colleagues to make a serious impression on the problems of crime in a community which, ideally, respects and understands what they are trying to do.

Determining, for instance, that the aim of the service is to reduce the risk of reoffending (as many services have done) is to place the staff who are able to influence offending behaviour by working directly with offenders, in the position of being the most important people in the service. The service is effective only to the extent that the staff whose task is to engage with the offender are committed to achieving change in the required direction. Of course the staff referred to here are not just probation officers; all staff who meet offenders whether at reception or in day centres or wherever, have their own contribution to make. No chief probation officer, no senior, nor unit manager can exert that influence. The manager's task and that of everyone else in the service who does not come face–to–face with offenders is to support, enable and empower the staff who do to exert their skills and abilities to best effect. The organisational chart in these circumstances, places the practitioners and those who meet and work with clients at the top of the organisational chart and the rest somewhere underneath.

So if the service's task in successfully challenging offending behaviour is best achieved by empowering offenders to take control and accept their own responsibility for their behaviour, and this in turn is best achieved by empowering practitioners to undertake their work with confidence and creativity, what does this imply about the role of management and the exercise of authority in the service? It is clear to me that it does not imply that frontline staff can be regarded as general practitioners operating in their own right and accountable only to themselves or to some wider notion of the profession. Professions have a poor record, being found to be more assiduous in the protection of their members than in the protection of the public. A model now so widely discredited will not do in a service which depends for its effectiveness on empowerment and the generation of creative practice developments on its practitioner staff. (In reality the 'general practitioner' model never really operated in the probation service because work has always been constrained to some extent by courts or committees, although there were certainly aspirations in the days when the medical model of practice was popular.) Nor does an empowerment model imply that managers are there simply to endorse the practice of the frontline workers and provide them with any resources they demand regardless of other considerations. Such a supine approach is the antithesis of management denying as it does the need for managers to provide leadership, to exercise accountability, to ensure the smooth running of the office, to contribute to the planning and policy development functions and to create a framework and a sense of purpose and direction within which staff can be enabled to deploy their skills and talents to maximum effect. The provision of these managerial components has only one purpose within an empowering environment, which is to maximise the contribution of frontline staff in their pursuit of effectiveness in empowering offenders to find and maintain crime free ways of living.

The empowerment of staff in their pursuit of effective practice is the primary task of the manager. However, the task is far from straight forward and requires the exercise of skill and judgement of a high order. For example, the identification of good practice itself is not without its problems and reference to objectives and service values alone will not solve them. The pursuit of good practice requires a dialogue between staff which takes account of values as well as service objectives sure enough. It also requires the testing of perceptions about appropriate goals and methods in each individual case. The decisions staff are required to make on a daily basis are often finely balanced, not lending themselves to easy and straight forward solutions. Without constant search for clarity of thought, staff can soon be drawn into the relativistic moral vacuum in which it is easy to collude with the client's view of reality and thus to miss the opportunities to challenge and move things on in a way which contributes to the empowering process. In supervision the manager has to be able to access these issues and to assist in the resolution of the many moral dilemmas which occur, thus releasing (empowering) the worker to operate effectively.

For many years there was a debate about the perceived problem of the combining in the same senior probation officer of the role of manager, with its stress on accountability and the role of casework consultant. It was felt that the officer would be unwilling to explore anxiety and weakness in someone who would ultimately be expected to write an appraisal or even a reference. Add to that concern serious doubts about the supervisory skills of the senior and it is easy to see why the debate was a lively one (and still is in some quarters). This debate can now be seen as reflecting the transition of the role of senior probation officer from that of *primus-inter-pares* to that of manager. The realisation that the manager's task is to ensure that effective supervision is afforded rather than necessarily carry it out personally, may be of some assistance in this case. There are good reasons for using the skills and experience of all the staff in the deliberations which surround the articulation of ideas about good practice as well as the resolution of problems relating to particular cases. The development of trust and the colleague support structures necessary for this require particular skills of managers. It also requires humility in the manager to be able to recognise that all the necessary skills do not reside in one place and to be open in working with staff to ensure the support arrangements operate effectively.

An empowering approach would take such issues in its stride, but the paradox must be faced. Empowerment implies the ceding of power. Taken to its logical conclusion, there is no room for doubt, would mean by definition the emasculation of the power of the worker by the offender, and the emasculation of the power of the manager by the worker. However, the resolution lies in the understanding that the tension generated by offenders wanting to do just as they would like without the constraints of the requirements of the order but are nonetheless contracted to do so (having agreed to be so bound) are reflected in the tensions generated by the worker wanting to operate outside the constraints of the organisational requirements but being none-theless contracted to do so (have agreed to join the service in the first place). Similarly the successful empowerment of the offender is without doubt signalled by a willingness to work within the constraints of the community (i.e. within the law) so the suc-cessful empowerment of the worker is signalled by a willingness to work within the constraints of the service's aims and priorities. However, it is now obvious that the chances of successful empowerment are substantially increased if there is a well understood and negotiated agreement about the roles and relationships involved. The proverb 'you can take a horse to water but you can't make it drink' may appear to reduce us all to equine docility, but there is a horse in all of us, managers and practi-tioners alike. Empowerment is the medium for ensuring that in our stubbornness we do not all die of thirst.

References

Audit Commission (1991) 'Going straight: developing good practice in the probation service', Occasional Paper 16.

Haxby, D. (1978) *Probation: A Changing Service*, Constable.

Home Office (1988) *Tackling Offending: an action plan*, HMSO.

Ross, R. R. (1990) *Time to Think: a cognitive model of offender rehabilitation and delinquency prevention*, University of Ottawa.

7 Management information systems in probation

Philip Whitehead

Introduction

From its origins in 1876 with the appointment of the first police court missionary, the probation service has experienced its share of diversification and change in areas of practice, philosophy and methods of working with clients. During the 1980s, particularly since 1984, the service has been affected by the attempts of successive Conservative administrations to control public expenditure in a climate of diminishing resources. More than ever before the service is having to demonstrate value for money (VfM) and that its performance is economical, efficient and effective (the solemn doctrine of the Three Es). In fact, since the early 1970s and the oil crisis which impacted adversely on the British economy, greater emphasis has been placed on the need for public sector organisations to use resources efficiently. This has led to a greater emphasis on the public sector being managed more rigorously, culminating in organisational policies, objectives, priorities and targets, and for information systems to measure performance against objectives.

Accordingly, what I want to do in the first section of this chapter is to explore how a number of changes during the last decade or so in one public sector organisation, namely the probation service, have influenced the development of management information system (MIS). In other words, and to borrow a phrase used by Garland (1985) when discussing the history of penal-welfare strategies, I want to explore the 'surface of emergence' of management information systems. Furthermore, this chapter will later explore, using a broad brush, a number of other significant features of information systems during the early 1990s.

Factors influencing the emergence of MIS: 1979 to the mid-1980s

During the first three years of Mrs Thatcher's first term in office, the Cabinet Office Efficiency Unit was established under Sir Derek Rayner. In fact, it was just five days after the 1979 General Election that Rayner was appointed by Mrs Thatcher as a special adviser on efficiency. His job was to improve efficiency and eliminate waste in numerous government departments which involved, by the end of 1983, 155 scrutinies and six government inter-departmental reviews (Humphrey, 1987, p. 91). These efficiency scrutinies, which concerned the promotion of managerial improvements in government and public sector departments, helped shape the Financial Management Initiative (FMI) which was launched on the 17th May 1982. The FMI evolved with the overall purpose of improving the management of government, but it is interesting to note that it was the Fulton Committee (Home Office, 1968) which gave the initial impetus to management accountability within the sphere of the civil service (Humphrey, 1987).

The underlying principles of the FMI are: economy, efficiency and effectiveness; a critical questioning of the role of the public sector; changing management practices to improve performance; greater accountability, cash limits and value for money; the setting of objectives, priorities and targets. Various government departments including the Department of Employment, Education and Science, Health and Social Security, and the Lord Chancellor's department, were required to examine their work and develop managerial responsibility, financial accounting and control. Therefore it is important to acknowledge that the emergence of the FMI during the early 1980s is associated with a variety of themes which included good management of resources and the development of management and financial management information systems.

Where the probation service is concerned it was the Statement of National Objectives and Priorities (SNOP), published in 1984, which was the document through which the principles of the FMI were first applied. Because I have discussed aspects of the SNOP document at length elsewhere (Whitehead, 1990a) it is unnecessary to be repetitive here. Suffice to say that SNOP was a watershed in the history of the service because it was the first ever statement by the Home Office which systematically articulated the objectives and priorities of the probation service in relation to five main task areas, in a way not previously attempted. Subsequently the fifty-six area probation services were expected to produce a Statement of Local Objectives and Priorities (SLOP) within the framework established by SNOP, the purpose of which was to articulate how the intentions of the national statement would be implemented at local area level.

Therefore, a number of changes affected the probation service during the first half of the 1980s. These changes, in turn, precipitated a much greater emphasis on financial accountability and the control of public sector spending, which meant the probation service had to face up to providing value for money and pay attention to the 3 Es. The FMI, SNOP and area SLOPs are important documents *per se*, but they are also important in the way they were the precursors of management information systems throughout the probation service.

The mid-1980s to 1989

On the 16th October 1986 E J Grimsey was appointed to examine the rationale of HM Inspectorate of Probation. The terms of reference were to review the objectives, powers and responsibilities of the Inspectorate and make recommendations to maximise the Inspectorate's impact on the economy, efficiency and effectiveness of the probation service, and the Inspectorate's contribution to the formulation of policy in the service and for an effective response to crime. It has already been clarified how, during the early 1980s, the probation service was being led by the nose in the direction of providing value for money. It is within this context that the work of the contemporary Inspectorate should be understood, because it has the job of helping area services to achieve national objectives and to ensure that areas are using their resources efficiently and performing effectively through both E and E and thematic inspections.

One of Grimsey's recommendations was to establish a working party on the development of performance indicators, defined as a tool which illuminates the effects of the actions or achievements of an organisation in pursuit of objectives. This is exactly what happened because a working party was established and met six times between June 1987 and March 1988. Its terms of reference included:

1. To identify aspects of performance which enables the Inspectorate to assess the effectiveness of area probation services

2. To identify those aspects of performance not covered by existing information, and consider what additional information should be collected

3. To take account of work already under way on FMIS (about which more will be said shortly).

Furthermore, performance indicators should be concerned with three things:

- the outputs and effectiveness of the service

- the inputs or resources used to obtain outputs i.e. the degree of economy in the use of resources

- the relationship between the above two points.

To develop performance indicators the working party dismantled SNOP clause by clause in the five key task areas which are:

1. Working with the courts.

2. Supervision in the community.

3. Throughcare and aftercare.

4. Community work.

5. Civil work.

In total 100 indicators were developed, but it should be acknowledged that a proper system of performance indicators depends upon appropriate information systems being available in local area services.

Whilst pursuing the development of performance indicators the Home Office was also working on establishing a Financial Management Information System (FMIS), which is principally concerned with resource management i.e. how much do different activities cost? In 1986 the Home Office commissioned a team of management consultants, Deloitte, Haskins and Sells, to create a FMIS for the probation service to ensure that the tax payer was getting value for money. By September 1988 the FMIS project team produced its first report on 'Producing a Functional Specification', which dealt with how the team proposed to tackle its task of producing a FMIS. The second report, which looked at the objectives and content of FMIS, was produced in January

1989. By March 1989 a third report was published. However, because the second report spelled out in some detail the objectives of a FMIS, these are worth reproducing in full as follows:

1. To enable area management and probation committees to monitor performance against area objectives.

2. To give managers the information to ensure that they are utilising resources economically.

3. To provide information which helps all staff to monitor and control resources, by enabling inputs to be related to expected and actual outcomes, so that appropriate responses can be made when plans and reality part company.

4. To provide information in accordance with 3. to enable devolution of responsibility and accountability to staff at all levels.

5. To provide information to HM Inspectorate and C6 Division to monitor resource use and area effectiveness.

6. To enable the Home Office to accurately cost specific probation activities.

7. To facilitate, at various levels, later evaluation of the usefulness of the effectiveness measures implied in 3.

By June 1989 a report on stage 3A was published which reinforced the rationale of the entire project by stating that:

a FMIS should provide integrated financial, activity and staff information in order to give probation committees, and managers within an area, the information needed to support policy planning and related budget development; to monitor performance against objectives and priorities; to provide information to ensure that resources are utilised in an effective, efficient and economic manner; to facilitate the development of delegated budgets, and to enable specific probation service activities to be costed.

Further changes, of a different nature, occurred towards the end of the 1980s because in July 1988 the Home Office produced its Green Paper on 'Punishment, Custody and the Community' which was followed by a White Paper. The legislative changes being proposed in these documents which are contained in the 1991 Criminal Justice Act (scheduled to be implemented during the autumn of 1992), will have important implications for probation information systems in the sense that the effects of these legislative changes will have to be monitored (see Giller, 1989, for an interesting paper on the monitoring implications of the new legislation).

This section should be concluded by referring to two other documents. The first is the Audit Commission Report on 'The Probation Service: Promoting Value for Money' (Audit Commission, 1989). In the first part of the report the Commission examines the role of the service in the wider criminal justice system. Part two proceeds to argue that probation officers must begin to supervise high risk offenders more effectively. To do this they must acquire the necessary skills and intervention must be properly assessed. The final part of the report states that better management systems are required to facilitate probation skills and methods of working. Accordingly further progress is required by managers of the service in six key areas, one of which is developing management information systems which should be simple, flexible and tuned to local targets and objectives.

The second report to mention is by the National Audit Office (NAO) which published 'Home Office: Control and Management of Probation Services in England and Wales' (National Audit Office, 1989). The NAO report focused on three main issues:

1. Whether the performance of the probation service is monitored against predetermined objectives and priorities.

2. Whether satisfactory arrangements exist to allocate funds to and control spending by, area services.

3. What is being done to promote an efficient and effective probation service.

Accordingly the report discusses the objectives and priorities of the probation service; future funding, control and financial management/monitoring information systems; and future training, inspections and performance indicators. This report emphasises the key role of management whose job is to ensure that resources are being used efficiently, to set objectives, priorities and targets, and to ensure the highest possible standards of performance. Unfortunately, argues the report, management skills have not kept pace with a rapidly changing, developing and expanding service.

Consequently a number of developments have occurred during the 1980s amongst which the most important are – FMI, SNOP, probation area SLOPs, the Grimsey report on the Inspectorate, the performance indicators working party reports, FMIS which is now referred to as RMIS (Resource Management Information

System – the software will be piloted during 1992), the Audit Commission and National Audit Office reports – which have influenced the emergence of management information systems in the probation service. In fact the nomenclature of the service has been expanded to incorporate a plethora of terms which are relatively new and mysterious to the uninitiated and include:

- MIRC - Management Information and Research Committee of ACOP

- SCIS - Home Office Standing Committee on Information Strategy

- NPRIE - National Probation Research and Information Exchange

- RMIS - Resource Management Information System

- PROBIS - Probation Information System

- PROBIS Contract Managers Group

- PROBIS Contract Steering Group

- PROBIS Operators Group

- CCCJS - Coordination of Computerisation in the Criminal Justice System

- CMS - Case Management System

Having now explored the surface of emergence of management information systems, the next section will look at the broad principles underlying these systems.

The principles of a management information system

Lucey (1987) defines a MIS as:

A system to convert data from internal and external sources into information and to communicate that information, in an appropriate form to managers at all levels in all functions to enable them to make timely and effective decisions for planning, directing and controlling the activities for which they are responsible (p.2).

Therefore a MIS translates data, which are raw facts and figures, into relevant and meaningful information which is then communicated to users. Lucey offers further clarification by saying that information is data which has been interpreted and understood by the recipient of the message. Or to put this another way, data are recorded facts and information is processed data which can be used as a basis for decision making (Ross, 1976, p.9). It is also helpful to conceptually differentiate between information systems and management information systems. According to Aron (1969) an information system provides knowledge, news, facts, data, learning and lore; by contrast a management information system provides managers within organisations with specific information to facilitate the process of planning, managing, resourcing, organising, decision–making and control. It is also needed to assess whether or not organisational objectives are being achieved.

Lucey emphasises the point that the information produced by a MIS should be relevant to the needs of the organisation. Consequently information should be useful to managers which has resulted in Zani (1970) commenting that 'an information system should be designed to focus on the critical tasks and decisions made within an organisation and to provide the kind of information that the manager needs to perform those tasks and make those decisions' (p. 221).

Furthermore Lucey says that information with the following six characteristics is more likely to be used within an organisation:

1. Timing - provide information to managers when they need it and in time to be used.

2. Appropriateness - it must be related to a manager's sphere of activity.

3. Accuracy - as far as possible information should be free from error and bias.

4. Detail - information should contain the least amount of detail consistent with effective decision making.

5. Frequency - the provision of regular outputs.

6. Understandability - if managers cannot understand the information then it is useless.

Although management information systems are an integral part of all modern organisations it should be understood that information is not an end in itself, but a means to an end which is determined by the rationale of the organisation. When creating a MIS the goal should not be to flood managers with information, even though there is a great temptation to do this in order to justify the existence of information staff. One of the problems of modern organisations is information overload, particularly where senior managers are concerned. Rather, the information provided must be as succinct as possible, yet providing managers with what is relevant to their sphere of operation and to assist them to strategically plan the future.

Prior to concluding this section it is helpful to conceptualise management information systems comprising six main building blocks which are delineated in the literature as:

1. Input - which concerns everything which enters the system and the methods for entering the data. It is vital to ensure accuracy and quality of data input.

2. Process/Analysis - which performs the transactional tasks by transforming data into quality information.

3. Output - concerns the eventual product, which can be in written, tabular and/or graphic format.

4. Technology - it is important to have the appropriate hardware platform and supporting software which ensures that the whole system works in the way intended.

5. Data Base - this is where all data needed to resource all users are stored.

6. Controls Block - concerns all those features which need to be designed into the system to ensure its smooth operation, which includes an information strategy, contingency plan, training for staff who use the MIS, back-up systems, housekeeping and security issues (Burch and Grudnitski, 1986).

Before summarising this brief excursion across the contours of management information systems, a word about computers is necessary because it appears that many people understand MIS solely in terms of a computer system. Lucey answers the question: are computers essential to MIS?, by saying:

> The short answer to this question is, not essential but they can be very useful. The study of MIS is not about the use of computers; it is about the provision and use of information relevant to the user. Computers are one – albeit important – means of producing information and concentration on the means of production rather than the needs of the user can lead to expensive mistakes (1987, p. 181).

To summarise some of the key concepts in the literature on MIS it may be said that a MIS must be related to the needs and specific objectives of the organisation; it must provide information which is relevant, meaningful and useful to managers at all levels within the organisation; it should facilitate the process of strategic planning, resourcing and decision making; ideally it should have six characteristics or key features. Importantly, a MIS is not an end in itself, but a means to an end. Accordingly 'a MIS has no intrinsic value of its own... the value of a MIS can only come from the users of the system, and not from the producers of the information' (Lucey, 1981, p.13). This is an important message which should prevent the emergence of an empire building mentality amongst information staff, because those involved in the information business exist to serve the wider needs of the organisation by providing a specific resource. Furthermore the provision and dissemination of information should be kept as succinct as possible; it has six main building blocks, and managers should be involved in the design of their organisation's MIS. With these concepts in mind the next section begins to explore the place of management information systems within the management process.

MIS and the management process

It has already been asserted that a MIS has no value in itself, no life of its own, nor an end in itself. Rather, information systems are a means to an end which is to measure performance against objectives. Therefore the starting point for a MIS must be for managers, in consultation with other members of staff, to articulate clear policies and objectives. Accordingly, the management process for the creation of a MIS should be located within the following paradigm.

First, each area service should produce a concise document which delineates policies and objectives. Senior managers should take the initiative to create the strategic framework within which its operations will be conducted, after consultation with the service as a whole. Therefore it is suggested that such a document will be produced every three to five years and should be a broad strategic statement of organisational aims, objectives and priorities.

Secondly, within this broad strategic policy framework, each service should produce an annual action plan. This is the document through which key objectives for the coming year will be articulated in specific areas of work in both field teams and specialist units.

Thirdly, it may be necessary to unpack the action plan to produce a number of achievement measurements (or performance indicators) which are the tools by which we measure performance against objectives. Therefore achievement measurements are logically related to and flow out of the action plan and seek to provide more precise measures of performance. To illustrate this I refer to the achievement measurements document produced by the Cleveland probation service during 1991 which articulated achievement measurements in a number of key areas of work. For example, where the supervision of offenders in the community is concerned, this document links wider service policy and action plan targets to achievement measurements as follows:

The policy of the service is to 'effectively supervise offenders who are subject to statutory orders by ensuring a range of appropriate provision and through the promotion of shared working' (Cleveland Probation Service, 1989).

Action plan targets

Target 2 - Offending behaviour must be addressed in every initial assessment and every supervision plan.

Target 3 - There will be a minimum of eight face–to–face contacts during the first three months, one of which should be a home visit. The first of these contacts must be within seven days of the commencement of the case.

Target 4 - Shared working through the use of in–service resource units and partnerships with other agencies.

Target 5 - The accommodation status of every offender will be checked.

Target 6 - The employment/education status of every offender will be checked.

Target 7 - Every offender supervised by the service will be invited to participate in a benefit check to ensure appropriate levels of benefit.

Achievement measurements

1. Speed of take–up of new orders.

2. Number of face to face home and office visits.

3. Number of failed contacts.

4. Evidence of contract between officer and client.

5. Evidence of shared working between probation officer, resource units, employment development officer, accommodation resources officer, welfare rights officers, volunteers and other agencies, where appropriate.

6. Evidence of addressing offending behaviour.

7. The number and proportion who received probation and

community service supervision with previous custody and previous supervision.

8. The number and proportion of first offenders who were placed on probation and community service supervision.

9. Number of offenders made the subject of an additional requirement and type.

10. Number who received various types of programmes via the statutory and voluntary resource units.

11. Number who successfully completed probation and community service orders.

12. Number who re–offend during the supervision period or who breached requirements.

Fourthly, once we have defined area policies, annual targets and achievement measurements, the next step is to create relevant information systems (consisting of research, routine monitoring, internal inspections, and action plan sampling) to provide specific information which will enable the service to measure performance against objectives and targets. Each service will have to consider which quantitative and qualitative data collection tools are required to elicit relevant information and also to consider appropriate manual and computer systems which support the process of data collection.

Finally, timescales are an important part of management process and planning. Working on the basis that the probation year duplicates the financial year of local authorities which begins in April suggests that every three years, in the month of January, the service should refine its broad policy document. Similarly, in January, but this time annually, the service should refine its action plan. Subsequently, each year during February and March, refinements will be made to achievement measurements and management information systems to ensure that relevant data are being collected. Figure 7.1 clarifies the component parts of the management process explained above.

Before considering other issues it may be observed that the words 'objective' and 'target' have been used above without qualification. In fact these two words are sometimes used interchangeably to mean the same thing, but this is a mistake. Therefore, it is necessary to inject some clarification into the way we talk about objectives and targets in the probation service.

	Components	Timescales
1.	Produce document on the organisation's policies and objectives. Broad strategic document.	During January to March, every 3 years.
2.	Produce Action Plan in key areas of work.	January each year.
3.	Produce Achievement Measurements document.	February to March each year.
4.	Develop and refine MIS to produce relevant information to measure performance against objectives.	February to March each year.

Figure 7.1

Objectives and targets

To have an objective is to have a goal. An objective is something that we wish to achieve and involves pursuing a particular course of action. For example, to proportionately reduce custodial sentences in a local criminal justice system is a laudable objective, so long as we know what the base line is before we begin to measure this objective.

By contrast, if we use the word target, whilst we may still talk legitimately about achieving a desired goal, there is something much more precise associated with the word target compared with objective. This is because a target may be accompanied by a specific target figure. Accordingly, to proportionately reduce custodial sentences by 2 per cent in a local criminal justice system during the coming year is a target, rather than an objective.

It is logical for an organisation like the probation service to state its objectives in broad terms as clearly as possible, because in doing so the organisation will be imbued with a sense of direction, purpose and shape. In an organisation which is responsible for a plethora of statutory and voluntary duties, it seems important to have some understanding of organisational objectives and goals. However, there are a number of issues we need to reflect upon when we move from objectives to specifying precise numerical targets.

First is the issue of how targets are arrived at. In my own area service we have wrestled for some time with the management process of setting appropriate targets in key areas of work. It must be ensured, as far as possible, that if numerical targets are formulated then they should be formulated by a scientific, objective and systematic process, and not arbitrarily. The danger is that if targets are formulated in an arbitrary fashion, they will have an air of unreality amongst staff. Furthermore, if targets are going to be set, then research and information staff have an important role to play within the management process to ensure both objectivity and realism.

Secondly, if targets are necessary because of the way we are having to manage the service during the 1990s, we must appreciate that an organisation like the probation service does not have complete control over target achievement. An area service may have targets of, for example, 1000 new community service orders and 500 Schedule 11 orders per year. Whilst there is no shortage of recommendations for these orders in cogently argued court reports prepared by probation officers, the courts do not always make decisions which are conducive to target achievement within the service. Therefore, because the service does not have total control over its working environment and therefore its workload, it may have difficulties reaching its targets in certain areas of work.

Thirdly, and this point is related to the second, all the criminal justice agencies within a local criminal justice system do not share the same primary task. In other words there is a lack of shared or common understanding between the probation service, police, courts, prison and crown prosecution service concerning the rationale of the criminal justice system, the aims of penal policy, and the way offenders should be dealt with.

It may therefore be argued that only if there is a common understanding between the main players operating within the criminal justice system, which would involve much greater coordination between the different agencies, would targets acquire real meaning. If we are going to operate with targets then they should be whole criminal justice system targets, rather than solely probation service targets. Only by operating in this way would it be possible, for example, to move towards realising Home Office aspirations for reducing custodial sentences.

Finally, targets set for different service operations could create unhealthy and misguided competition between, say, community service and probation orders. If it appears that the community service unit will not attract 1000 new orders this year and if probation orders with a Schedule 11 requirement will be 100 orders short of the target figure of 500, it would be unhelpful to see staff from both units competing with each other. Instead, different units within the probation service should be cooperating with each other to ensure that each unit deals with appropriate clients, rather than competing for the same market of clients.

Consequently it would be helpful for each area service and local criminal justice system to clarify its policies, objectives and targets for the use of different disposals, so that a particular type of offender would be considered suitable for community service and another type for probation with Schedule 11. In fact this will be a critical issue for local criminal justice systems when the 1991 Criminal Justice Act is introduced, because we will need to match more closely than we do at present different orders (probation, probation with requirements, community service, and the new combined order) with particular types of offenders (for more information see Whitehead, 1992).

To summarise, if numerical targets are specified in an arbitrary fashion; if the service has little control over target achievement because of decisions made by other criminal justice agencies; if it would be more logical to have whole criminal justice system targets rather than probation service targets only; and if targets create misguided competition between different service operations which could indicate the lack of a clear policy, then we must be very careful about how targets are introduced and used.

However, having said all this, the document produced by HM Inspectorate on *Efficiency and Effectiveness Inspections in the Probation Service: the First Year* (1990a) looks at different ways the word target can be used:

- it could mean a probation team focussing on a particular client group such as those at risk of custody

- it could mean achieving something by a specific date such as the introduction of a risk of reconviction scale

- or it could mean something as precise as reducing custodial sentences by 'n' percent by such a date.

Moreover, the notion of operational targets is related to the increasingly important concept of resource levels in a cash limited environment. This means that, based upon staffing resources allocated to a particular sphere of service delivery (i.e. community service) it is expected that a specific number of orders will be achieved during the coming year. If the target is not reached there are obvious implications for resource allocation in future. It should also be acknowledged that operational targets have implications for probation officers within field teams because community service, for example, will not be able to reach its target of new orders unless they are recommended by probation officers in their court reports. Consequently, operational targets have implications for the principle of shared working between specialist units and fieldwork operations.

There is also the notion of practice targets which specify, for example, how many contacts probation staff should have with clients during the first three months of a probation order (for a more comprehensive discussion of targets see Statham above, Chapter 4).

Having taken a detour to consider a number of issues associated with objectives and targets which are pertinent at the present time, I will now move on to look at other issues.

Critical success factors

At times the probation service feels like an unwieldy organisation because of the diverse range of tasks it has to perform. In fact the Jarvis Manual (Weston, 1987) delineates thirty-five mandatory duties and a further six 'other' duties. If each area service produced information in any detail on a total of forty-one duties then it would very quickly experience information overload, which must be avoided. Moreover, despite the importance of creating a system of achievement measurements or performance indicators in key areas of work, it should be acknowledged that in Cleveland, for example, we have over 105 achievement measurements (Cleveland Probation Service, 1991) which results in the production of a large amount of information each year. Consequently some thought should be given to what may be described as critical success factors within an organisation. The thinking behind this notion is to select a handful of key areas of activity in which we want to succeed and on which to provide information. I suggest the following critical success factors for consideration.

Firstly, at the input–court stage of service operation, one measure of success is the number and proportion of offenders, who are considered to be at risk of custody, being diverted from custody into community supervision programmes. A risk of custody scale is a gatekeeping instrument which can assist in measuring the degree of success in this area of work and thus provides important management information. However, existing risk of custody scales will have to be amended in the light of the 1991 Criminal Justice Act which puts greater emphasis on current offence seriousness rather than previous convictions when determining sentence.

Secondly, at the stage where a court order is in operation, one success factor could be the level of contact between the probation officer and the client. For example, action plan target 3 on levels of contact (Cleveland Probation Service, 1991) states that 'In every new community supervision case, including post-release, there will be a minimum of eight face to face contacts by the supervising officer in the first three months, one of which should be a home visit. These contacts will be in addition to contacts with other service personnel'.

Thirdly, at what may be described as the output stage of service operation, reconviction rates should be considered as another measure of success. It may be argued that, over the last few years, the service has lost its way in the sense of forgetting that one of its main functions is crime reduction. Instead of focusing on the impact of probation officers on offending behaviour, i.e. output measure of effectiveness, the service has become preoccupied with input measures. Therefore, a reconviction predictor scale may be used to drag the service back to output measures (Humphrey *et al.*, 1991) and to those probation officers who appear more effective than others at reducing offending behaviour. Consequently I consider there are benefits for the probation service in specifying a limited number of areas of probation activity in which it wants to succeed. This has implications for the future design of information systems.

Current developments in information strategies

At the time of writing this chapter the important developments affecting information systems within the probation service were RMIS, Coordination of Computerisation in the Criminal Justice System (CCCJS) and Case Management System (CMS), about which more should be said at this point. Reference has already been made above to FMIS which is now referred to as RMIS. In October 1990 a document called 'Towards Managing RMIS into Practice' stated that 'The Resource Management Information System is a tool, provided by the Home Office, which draws together a number of current initiatives and is designed to assist each probation service in the task of managing the resources of their Organisation to best meet the demands made of it'. RMIS is fundamentally about ensuring that individual probation areas use limited resources economically, efficiently and effectively, and that value for tax payer's money is being provided. These will be critical issues from April 1992 when a system of cash limits is introduced.

Subsequently Wakefield, in a paper he produced in February 1991, clarified the components of RMIS when he said that in phase 1 the 'core' RMIS will be able to manipulate and analyse information from other systems – principally personnel, finance and case management systems – in order to evaluate the effectiveness and efficiency of service delivery and to plan the allocation of resources. By phase 2, which will 'permit more detailed evaluation of service and unit effectiveness at cost centre level', it will be important that area services have created cost centres; established criminal and civil report monitoring systems; use risk of custody and risk of reconviction scales; have case record systems which provide aggregated information for managers and practitioners on clients. Consequently RMIS is an important development within the probation service which makes use of existing information systems to provide information on the costs of different functions.

Next, is the CCCJS development which is:

> concerned to promote co–operative working and automatic information exchange between the criminal justice agencies in order to improve the accuracy, timeliness and availability of information. As well as improving value for money in the criminal justice process, the resulting reduction in delays should lead to less distress to defendants, victims and their families. Not least, it should result in shorter periods of remand (Pape, 1991, p.45).

In theory this sounds a good idea and a step in the right direction. However, we must bear in mind that computer developments within the different criminal justice agencies have, over the last few years, occurred independently of each other which has resulted in limited compatibility. Moreover, during the next few years different computer systems will be installed throughout the criminal justice system such as MASS in the Magistrates' Courts, CREST in the Crown Court, SCOPE in the Crown Prosecution Service and LIDS within the prison service. Nevertheless it is hoped to establish a pilot project which would link these different computer systems in one area of the country between 1992 and 1995 (Pape, 1991, p.45). It should also be acknowledged that the probation service could end up with a new computerised case management system during the 1990s, which will now be considered.

In April 1991 C6 Division at the Home Office published 'Towards an Integrated Information Strategy'. This paper made it clear that the Home Office would like to see a more integrated and coherent approach to information technology. This is currently prevented by the fact that forty out of fifty-five area probation services use PROBIS computer software, whilst the remaining fifteen have their own local variations on a common theme. Even though PROBIS may be terminally ill the death rattle could be heard for some time to come which leads one to ask: what system should replace PROBIS? It is acknowledged that it makes good sense for all probation areas to use the same case management system. Consequently six systems have been evaluated (at Cambridgeshire, Greater Manchester, Hereford and Worcester, Merseyside, Mid–Glamorgan and Northumbria) and there may well be quite a dog fight before a decision is made concerning which CMS will be installed in all fifty-five probation areas during the 1990s.

It may therefore be argued that a MIS strategy for the 1990s must take cognizance of the debates on having one integrated and coherent CMS; the intention to coordinate information technology throughout the criminal justice system; and the issue of costs which is the business of RMIS. Furthermore an information technology strategy for the probation service must ensure that it supports criminal and civil report monitoring, risk of custody scales, risk of reconviction scales, and delivers information on offenders from the beginning for their orders through to completion. We must also have compatible hardware and software systems which are able to produce monthly, quarterly and annual performance reports to measure performance against objectives. A management information system must be able to produce information on the costs of different probation activities and we must ensure that each local service has properly trained staff to operate the information system efficiently. It must be said that, at the present time, developments associated with information systems and computerisation appear quite daunting and overwhelming.

Some concerns

In December 1990 HM Inspectorate of Probation published the results of its inspection of information and computer strategies (HM Inspectorate of Probation, 1990b). It touched upon a number of issues already considered in this chapter when it recommended that information outputs must be directly related to objectives and targets; the service must clarify what information is required, why, when, where, for whom and how; the relationship between manual and computer systems should be clarified; prior to devising and implementing an information strategy it is important to create a management culture, facilitate the notion of management information as a resource, and to ensure that data inputs are reliable and accurate.

Whilst all these recommendations may be deemed highly

praiseworthy, it is important to state that the most sophisticated and well designed MIS will not be able to capture or measure all dimensions of probation work which probation staff undertake. There are many features of probation work undertaken each day by probation officers, which are of value to clients, the criminal justice system and wider community, yet which are hidden from the public gaze and therefore beyond precise quantitative and qualitative measurement. How, for instance, do we measure that a lonely and isolated client has been befriended by a probation officer? How do we adequately capture the help and support given to clients at a time in their lives when they have been rejected by family and friends? How do we measure the provision of emotional and psychological support, the gesture of friendship and care? How do we measure the ceaseless efforts of probation officers made on behalf of clients and the much needed exercise of discretion, flexibility and tolerance, which helps clients to complete court orders? And what have our information systems to say about the political, socio-economic climate created by the New Right since 1979 which has contributed to inequality, unemployment, deprivation, poverty and the creation of an underclass, which deeply affects the lives of many clients and with which probation officers have to cope (Field, 1989). Consequently, as I have argued elsewhere 'many features of probation work are beyond precise quantitative and qualitative calculation and it is worth stating that both the courts and society would be less human and greatly impoverished if probation officers were not engaged in these activities' (Whitehead, 1990b, p.36).

In the thrust towards implementing the 3Es and achieving VfM during the 1990s, we should not lose sight of the fact that there are a number of important features of probation work which cannot be measured, and some which can only present part of the picture (ACOP, 1989). Moreover, in striving to be more efficient and to live within a cash limited budget the probation service and other human service organisations will have to be very careful that they do not end up knowing the price of everything and the value of nothing, to use one of Oscar Wilde's incisive one-liners.

Summary and conclusion

This chapter has attempted to provide a broad overview of and to explore a number of pertinent issues related to management information systems in the probation service, namely: the surface of emergence of management information systems; the major principles underlying the creation of a MIS within an organisation; the location of information systems in the management process; issues associated with objectives and targets; critical success factors; current developments associated with RMIS, CCCJS and CMS; and some concerns associated with the development of MIS.

It is clear that throughout the fifty-five probation areas much greater emphasis has been put on developing a managerial culture during the last few years and, concomitantly, the creation of information systems to demonstrate accountability and measure performance against managerially defined objectives. It may be positively argued that such developments have produced greater clarity in the probation service because it now has more understanding of what, as an organisation, it is trying to achieve, which in turn can be measured and demonstrated by management information systems. The service must now move on from producing and disseminating information, to using information in order to imaginatively develop policy and practice; maintain high standards of practice and the achievement of excellence by illuminating those areas of service delivery which can be improved; distribute workloads more equitably amongst staff; contribute to staff supervision, development and appraisal; make effective resource bids; make the best use of current resources. But let me conclude by sounding a note of caution from a theologian and then a historian.

During the 1970s the theologian Hans Kung talked about efficiency posing a threat to man's humanity and man losing himself in the anonymous mechanisms, techniques, powers and organisations of an efficiency-oriented society. He stated that life today is 'thoroughly organised, fully regulated, bureaucratised and rapidly becoming computerised from morning to night' (Kung, 1977, p. 585). Furthermore, the historian Lawrence Stone (1987) says that modern man walks a knife edge between the rational and the emotional, and where the former is concerned says there is:

> a 'technetronic' society, smooth, impersonal, rational, and scientific, a kind of universal IBM company ruled over by the computer. While it can be supremely efficient, it is also drab and sterile, leaving no place either for the emotions, including the finer ones of love and compassion, or for the sense of aesthetic mystery and wonder which is at the root of all great literatures, art, and music (p. 198).

From our vantage point in the 1990s it may be perceived that we have become more bureaucratised, computerised, and that the notion of efficiency is assuming the cachet of a new religion. Therefore, we do well to remind ourselves that the probation service exists to provide a service to people, and at its best is the humane and caring face of local criminal justice systems in its work with individual offenders, even though it will have to diversify during the 1990s (Harris, 1992). In searching to develop management information systems within an organisation which has adopted a managerially oriented culture, we must not forget that the probation service should continue to help and support offenders in a variety of ways and that organisational and managerial developments should facilitate the achievement of this objective.

Accordingly, we should not become overly captured by the prevailing fashion of the doctrine of the 3Es, VfM, latest technology and information (because it is a fact of history that all doctrines and fashions come and go) even though they should be treated seriously and with respect. When all is said and done these are mere instruments playing incidental music, and the means to a much greater end, which is the provision of a public and humane service to a vulnerable section of the community. For without the probation service the work of the criminal justice system cannot be truly just (Temple, 1934).

References

ACOP (1989) 'Financial management information system: response to stage 3A report'. Finance and Resource Use Group, 30.10.89.

Aron, J.D. (1969) 'Information systems in perspective', in G.B. Davis and G.C. Everest (eds) (1976), *Readings in Management Information Systems*, McGraw-Hill.

Audit Commission (1989) *The Probation Service: Promoting Value for Money*, HMSO.

Burch, J.G., and Grudnitski, G. (1986, 4th edition) *Information Systems: Theory and Practice*, John Wiley.

Cleveland Probation Service (1989) Future Directions: Objectives and Priorities.

Cleveland Probation Service (1991) Action Plan 1991.

Field, F. (1989) *Losing Out: The Emergence of Britain's Underclass*, Blackwell.

Garland, D. (1985) *Punishment and Welfare: A History of Penal Strategies*, Gower.

Giller, H. (1989) 'Systems management and monitoring', in H. Rees and E.H. Williams (eds) (1989) *Punishment, Custody and the Community: Reflections and Comments on the Green Paper*, STICERD.

Harris, R. (1992) *Crime, Criminal Justice and the Probation Service*, Tavistock/Routledge.

HM Inspectorate of Probation (1990a) *Efficiency and Effectiveness Inspection in the Probation Service: The First Year*, HMSO.

HM Inspectorate of Probation (1990b) *Information and Computer Strategies*, HMSO.

Humphrey, C. (1987) *The Implications of the FMI for the Probation Service*, Department of Accounting and Finance, University of Manchester.

Humphrey, C., Carter, P. and Pease, K. (1991) *A Reconviction Predictor for*

Probationers, Departments of Accounting and Social Policy, University of Manchester.

Kung, H. (1977) *On Being a Christian,* Collins.

Lucey, T. (1981, 4th edition) *Management Information Systems,* D.P. Publications.

Lucey, T. (1987, 5th edn) *Management Information Systems,* D.P. Publications.

National Audit Office (1989) *Home Office: Control and Management of Probation Services in England and Wales,* HMSO.

Pape, R. (1991) 'Coordination of computerisation in the criminal justice system', Research Bulletin No. 30, Home Office Research and Statistics Department.

Ross, J.E. (1976) *Modern Management and Information Systems,* Reston.

Stone, L. (1987) *The Past and the Present Revisited,* London.

Temple, W. (1934) *The Ethics of Penal Action,* The Clarke Hall Fellowship.

Weston, W.R. (1987) *Jarvis's Probation Officers' Manual* (4th edn), Butterworth.

Whitehead, P. (1990a) *Community Supervision for Offenders: A New Model of Probation,* Avebury.

Whitehead, P. (1990b) *Management Information Systems in Probation: A Cleveland Perspective,* Social Work Monograph No. 92, Norwich.

Whitehead, P. (1992) *Alternatives to Custody and a Presentence Report Matrix: Some implications of the 1991 Criminal Justice Act,* Cleveland Probation Service, unpublished.

Zani, W.M. (1970) 'Blueprint for MIS', in G.B. Davis and G.C. Everest (eds) (1976) *Readings in Management Information Systems,* McGraw-Hill.

8 Information systems and management strategy

Philip Whitehead

Introduction

The previous chapter on management information systems attempts to provide a wide ranging overview of a sphere of work which has become important in the probation service. It could best be described as a bird's–eye view of the subject. However, it is now necessary to be more specific in this supplementary chapter by providing a worm's–eye view of a management strategy (and I am putting a broad construction on the word strategy) for management information systems.

All area probation services, in one form or another, have members of staff who are involved in the production, analysis, interpretation and dissemination of information. In Cleveland, for example, the Information Unit comprises an Information Manager, Information Assistant and Computer Operator, in addition to secretarial support. As was made clear in the previous chapter, the provision of information by information unit staff must be located within a corporate management strategy which embraces the organisation's policies, objectives and targets. Furthermore, an information unit should have its own strategy (as should all teams and specialist units), an example of which is now presented for consideration.

Information strategy for an area probation service

Without proper information, efficient and effective management is impossible (HM inspectorate of Probation, 1990)

The Information Unit was established in response to the proper requirement that the Cleveland Probation Service should be able to demonstrate its performance in achieving its planned objectives, with full account being taken of all public resources employed in that process. This development has, of necessity, had to take place against a background of a service coming to learn how to make the best use of information. As this learning takes place there is also a requirement to plan for new initiatives, such as the Resource Management Information System (RMIS), which aims to enhance our public accountability and effectiveness in the use of all the resources allocated to the service. In developing this strategy it is of critical importance to note that information encompasses the production of statistical material, its effective presentation and analysis, as well as the provision of conclusions and recommendations. Accordingly, the results we seek to achieve are:

Target 1   The production and supply of information which accurately demonstrates service performance, in relation to all of its activities which originate from the courts of criminal and civil jurisdiction.

Target 2   The production and supply of information which will assist the Probation Committee and service managers in the process of planning for the deployment and use of resources to achieve formulated targets.

Target 3   To ensure the efficient and comprehensive collation of all relevant information which will assist in demonstrating performance and planning for the deployment and use of resources.

Target 1

The production and supply of information which accurately demonstrates service performance, in relation to all of its activities which originate from the courts of criminal and civil jurisdiction.

1. The information unit will ensure the production of an annual report which demonstrates service performance

against its planned targets. These targets will relate to the activities of the service which originate from the courts of criminal and civil jurisdiction. In the production of this report the fullest attention will be paid to the effective use of statistical and other data with the aims of ensuring accuracy, readability and the promotion of interest in the work of the service.

2. On a quarterly basis the information unit will provide performance reports concerning service activities in these key areas. Such reports will make use of an established set of performance indicators drawn from Form 20 and 30 data bases as well as SIR monitoring. There will also be an appraisal of performance against previous quarterly periods, paying attention to any discernible trends. The scope of comparative analysis will be determined in association with the Headquarters' group.

3. Whole service quarterly performance reports will be made available to all other service managers and personnel as required.

4. The information unit will ensure the supply of quarterly performance information to all those service units which are dependent upon it for the processing and analysis of their statistical material. Such reports concerning the performance of each unit will be based on an agreed set of performance indicators drawn from Form 20, 30 and SIR monitoring forms.

5. The information unit will ensure the production of information on a monthly basis concerning the workload of fieldwork and specialist units in regard to existing workload and throughput for the previous month.

6. On behalf of the designated ACPO with responsibility for Internal Monitoring and Inspection (IMI), the information unit will ensure the effective coordination and design of the IMI programme.

7. The information unit will ensure the rapid publication of the results of internal inspections. Such reports will not only reflect performance against service targets in the identified area for inspection, but will also reflect the process and cost of the inspection.

8. The information unit will undertake other planned sampling exercises which the Headquarters' group deem necessary in order to demonstrate service performance in relation to any formulated targets.

9. The information unit will ensure the publication of the results of any research activity, within which the service has participated, and which will assist in illuminating and improving any aspect of service performance.

Target 2

The production and supply of information which will assist the Probation Committee and service managers in the process of planning for the deployment and use of resources to achieve formulated targets. In the pursuit of this target it is accepted that the achievement of Target 1, that is the demonstration of service performance, will be the cornerstone of future resource planning. The following activities are aimed at ensuring the completion of the information units part in that task:

1. The information unit will aim to ensure the rapid identification of trends regarding the intake and processing of work originating from the courts of criminal and civil jurisdiction. Where such trends indicate either an under or over use of service resources, that matter will be brought to the attention of the responsible divisional ACPO and the Headquarters' group as soon as possible.

2. The information unit will seek to assist the future planning for the deployment and use of service resources, through the provision of planned Information Bulletins, which focus upon the predicted local impact on resource allocation and service operational practices, of legislation and central directions.

3. The information unit, through the seeking out and supply of appropriate information, will assist in the development of sanctioned service activities.

4. The information unit will ensure effective liaison and joint work with the Finance and Personnel units, especially in the development of RMIS and in the provision of all relevant information which assists the functioning of these units.

Target 3

To ensure the efficient and comprehensive collation of all relevant information which will assist in demonstrating performance and for the deployment and use of resources.

1. The information unit will seek to develop the information gathering systems of all fieldwork and specialist operational

units, with the aim of ensuring relevance, accuracy and usefulness in demonstrating performance and future planning. This will require a programme of review with all appropriate unit personnel.

2. The information unit will seek to ensure that all service managers are resourced to make the best use of information. The achievement of this aim will require the provision of a planned programme which seeks to educate staff in the use of statistical information and teach the accessing of information from computer terminals.

3. The information unit will continue to develop the service's achievement measurements (performance indicators) and while this activity will again pay attention to relevance and usefulness, it will also take account of planned change resulting from legislation.

4. The information unit will ensure the implementation of a developing strategy in regard to the use of new technology in operational units. In particular the unit will ensure that staff are trained to access Form 20, 30, SIR monitoring and other relevant performance information, and that it is able to provide a consultancy service which is concerned with the best use of all software.

5. The information unit will ensure the rapid communication concerning alterations in statistical collation requirements, and will provide advice to ensure the fullest understanding of such changes when they do occur.

6. The information unit will seek to develop a coordinated, well trained and motivated team. This will be achieved by the following:

    ● the publication within the service of the programme of unit activities and the consultancy which can be offered

    ● regular meeting of all unit staff

    ● the individual supervision of all staff

    ● a planned programme of training for staff, as required, to implement this strategy.

Within an organisation which has clothed itself with a more managerially oriented culture since the early 1980s, illustrated by the development of organisational policies, objectives and targets, it is important for the probation service to clarify the rationale of management information systems and to articulate a clear, all embracing, information unit strategy. However, in addition to each area service having an information unit strategy along the lines suggested above, we should also consider the suggestion that such an area strategy should be located within a wider national strategy. What I mean by this may be explained by saying that during 1984 the Home Office produced a Statement of National Objectives and Priorities (SNOP) for the probation service, and it was within this nationally determined framework that each area service began to develop a Statement of Local Objectives and Priorities (SLOP). Similarly, it may be argued that the probation service requires a Statement of National Information Strategy (SNIS) within which each area service can begin to articulate a Statement of Local Information Strategy (SLIS).

When I came into the burgeoning information business in 1987 it was apparent that there was no obvious route towards becoming a properly trained information manager. Because of the lack of a national structure for the training and development of information unit staff within a rapidly changing and developing organisation, it is not surprising that my own job developed on an *ad hoc* basis. Moreover, Godson and Cureton (1990) in their enquiry into the role and status of research and information staff discovered a considerable degree of 'ad hocery'. They found that research and information staff throughout the fifty-five area services are known by different titles, are paid different salaries for doing similar work, and only nine out of forty-five heads of information units attend the chief officer's team meetings as of right. Therefore, there is a lack of consistency amongst area services concerning the role, function, status and place of information staff within their organisation and the management process. However, if, as Godson and Cureton argue, information staff should move centre stage to become an integral component in the management process and be involved in translating management strategies into area, team and individual officer objectives, these staff require training to assume these responsibilities.

To some degree it is inevitable that the provision and dissemination of information will reflect local conditions, which is right and proper. Increasingly, though, there is merit in considering the development of information units during the 1990s which have the task of providing management information, within the context of a national coordinated strategy. In July 1991 Frank Smith, of the Home Office Probation Service Division, addressed the NPRIE General Meeting. Towards the end of his address he asked the assembled information officers a number of pertinent questions which included:

> What ought to be their role? How far do you feel involved in the policy making process within your services? Are you given

enough feedback from managers and main grade officers about the usefulness of the information you provide? Is Home Office assistance needed, and if so, where, when and how? (Smith, 1991, p4).

My answer to the last question is that Home Office assistance is required to coordinate the work of information and research staff throughout the probation service, which is currently pre-occupied by thinking about case management systems, the cost of activities and local inspection programmes. Assistance is required to develop relevant performance indicators, critical success factors, the achievement of greater consistency in the production and dissemination of information, and the use of risk of custody and risk of reconviction scales, to ensure that hybrid and *ad hoc* systems are pulled together under the umbrella of a national strategy. The components of such a national strategy should take cognizance of the following:

1. We need to clarify the role, function and status of all staff who work with area service information units.

2. We must be more clear about the rationale and parameters of information unit work.

3. We must clarify what information unit staff should be called (Godson and Cureton, 1990, p6).

4. We must clarify the contribution information unit staff can make to the management process.

5. Training is critical (and here I attempt to answer the 'how' part of Smith's last question).

It is now incomprehensible that there are specific training courses for newly appointed probation officers, senior probation officers and assistant chief probation officers, but no such nationally coordinated course for those who have overall responsibility for information units. This is a deficiency which requires urgent rectification, given the way in which the organisation is evolving. Furthermore, such training for heads of information units would need to encompass a variety of issues which include:

- understanding the culture of the probation service in the 1990s

- acquiring knowledge of management culture and process

- how to manage oneself and information unit staff

- how to supervise and appraise information unit staff

- managing the production and supply of information
- how to write statistical reports combining text, tables and graphs
- the presentation of information to different audiences
- how to contribute to the management process and strategic thinking
- the effective use of new technology
- relating the concepts of economy, efficiency, effectiveness, and value for money, to the production of information
- links with finance and personnel
- how to train the organisation, at all level, to make the best use of information to measure performance against objectives, maintain the highest standards of corporate performance and achieve best practice.

These training issues, which could be pursued within the context of a nationally coordinated training programme (but perhaps delivered at a regional level through the creation of appropriate regional structures), must be taken seriously if the probation service wants to establish well trained information unit staff who are able to contribute constructively to managing the service, by providing management information, in an emergent management oriented culture.

References

Godson, D. and Cureton, L. (1990) *Management, Information and Research,* NPRIE.

HM Inspectorate of Probation (1990) *Information and Computer Strategies,* Home Office.

Home Office (1984) *Probation Service in England and Wales: Statement of National Objectives and Priorities,* HMSO.

Smith, F.J. (1991) *The Place for Research In Assembling Definitions of Good Practice Standards,* Address to NPRIE General Meeting on 16.7.91.

9 Corporate management in probation

Roger Shaw

> We are going to win and the Industrial West is going to lose
> because for you the essence of management is getting ideas out
> of the heads of bosses into the heads of labour. For us the core
> of management is the art of mobilising and putting together
> the intellectual resources of all employees in the services of the
> firm.

So said Matsuchita, a senior Japanese manager in 1985, as he
indicted American and European organisations for their lack of
effective team management (Margerison and McCann, 1990).

The probation service has a history of initiatives with origins in
the intellectual resources of main grade officers. Whilst sometimes
these developments stood alone, to wither and die when the driving
force behind them left for another post – a feature particularly
marked in respect of probation service work with the
community – others have been well managed and, where
appropriate, absorbed into the practice of services (Henderson,
1987; HM Inspectorate of Probation, 1990). Additionally, many
of the new ideas grown from the grass roots have blossomed and
seeded elsewhere.

This state of affairs is changing, firstly because of increasing
emphasis on modern western management principles, and
secondly because of greater direction from the Home Office as it
exercises its right as principal funder to say, in effect, 'He who
pays the piper calls the tune' (Home Office, 1991). The risk from
these changes is that instead of leading to more effective management of new initiatives the double grip could stifle them as both

resources in general and management time in particular become available only for those developments which sustain the political and pragmatic imperatives of the day. The increasing size of management structures, unless accompanied by concomitant refinements and improvements in communication and, most importantly, philosophy, risk 'ideas' as Matsuchita called them, coming only from the bosses and no longer from the intellectual resources of all employees. If that happened it would shift the service from being one of the most innovative organisations in the criminal justice system – which history confirms whatever its critics may say – to what Matsuchita would see as a further example of western management philosophy; a philosophy which has been shown to be wanting. Matsuchita was indicting team management in western industrial organisations, much of whose labour might not be expected to have the depth of intellect and education which is to be found in the probation service. How much greater is the loss to the probation service if the intellectual resources of its staff are not mobilised in the service of the organisation.

The push from government during the 1980s and early 1990s has been towards stronger management (Home Office 1990, 1991) – but what does this term imply? To many main grade officers and senior probation officers it means, or if it does not mean it results in, an increasing amount of instruction and direction from above, with lessening opportunity for ideas to be pushed up from below. The agenda of management meetings are thus taken over by top management issues with little space for shop floor developments and initiatives. Greater constraints placed upon staff to work within tighter frameworks risk leading to reduced opportunity for the mobilisation of the intellectual resources of all employees. The whole service thus becomes less influential in the development of the strategy to be adopted for the attainment of objectives as this is increasingly dictated from elsewhere. However, unless we accept that management has a monopoly of ideas – surely an absurd assumption – it is imperative that the developing structures in services ensure that the maximum intellectual resources are mobilised and not choked. There is a wide gulf between an unmanaged group doing its own thing which some political persuasions within the service have supported in the past, and management managing in ways which use to the full the initiative, creativity and innovative spirit which have always been present in the service. Yet in his study of change in the probation service, May (1991) found that whilst managers had some optimism about the future, front line staff were largely pessimistic about developments and what the future held. This gulf in morale and expectation between management and front line is worrying and does not augur well for the service in the future if it is not resolved.

Nowadays we know much more about *what* is happening in the probation service, thanks largely to the development of crude performance indicators and the availability of information technology but we still know relatively little about *why*. Easterby–Smith *et al.* (1991) suggest that qualitative research into management has taken second place to quantitative methods and as a result there has been a lack of understanding as to *why* things happen as distinct from *what* is happening. They point out that 'management is essentially about controlling, influencing and structuring the awareness of others. It is the central process whereby organisations achieve the semblance of coherence and direction' (p.81). It is thus unlikely in commerce and industry that the influential and the powerful will agree to research, the results of which may not conform to their hidden agenda and political imperatives. Easterby–Smith *et al.* conclude 'the more powerful members of society generally have both the awareness and the means to protect themselves from the prying eyes and tape recorders of researchers. It is rare to find researchers who have succeeded in studying powerful members of society without adopting methods of deceit, concealment and subterfuge' (p.82). Gummesson (1988) posed the question, 'What real opportunities does an academic researcher have to understand what is going on in a company?' He concluded 'They are very limited, particularly in relation to the complex process of decision–making, implementation and change'. Industrial and commercial managements are not alone in this respect. Many examples can be found in criminal justice, for instance the refusal of the then Lord Chief Justice to permit Andrew Ashworth's research into the Judiciary following publication of the report on the pilot study (Ashworth, 1984). It is beyond refute that most criminal justice research, and social research generally, has been carried out on weak and uninfluential sections of society. Easterby–Smith *et al.* (1991) quote Taylor and Bogan (1984) to support this contention and Slater (1989) confirms that it is the mad, bad, sad and ill who are mostly the subject of social science study. It is not surprising, therefore, that in relation to management in criminal justice, as in industry and commerce, whilst research shows *what* is happening, it usually fails to show *why*. The hypothesis of this paper is that this extends to the probation service as it embraces modern western management techniques and places increasing importance on performance indicators. It is important to emphasise here that this paper is not an attack on management by objectives nor on the targeting of

outputs – quite the reverse – but with the important rider that
those who really believe in Matsuchita's concept of putting
together the intellectual resources of all employees in the services
of the firm need to know *why* things happen and need to have
involved all staff in those happenings. The key issue, therefore, is
how to use the increased managerial resource which has become
available during the past few years and the focus being given by
the Home Office, in a way which can enable the intellectual
resources of all employees to be mobilised and put together in
furtherance of the objectives of the service. Partly this is about
adequate communication systems and partly it is about training,
touched on later in this chapter, but in the main it is about
management style and philosophy. A style of management which
uses the intellectual resources of the management team to decide
policy and then tells staff what to do results in ideas being
available from only a small proportion of the total intellectual
resources of the organisation. Many members of staff will have
knowledge and experience which is not available to management
and consequently will not inform decisions. Is this not a waste of
intellectual resources?

Alternatively management might tap the resources of its staff
in order to gain information on a particular subject. As an example
one can take working parties, used widely in probation services to
undertake specific pieces of work. However, what is the value in
the establishment of, for instance, cross grade working parties if
the service is structured in such a way that working party partici-
pation is simply a voice in response to the ideas of management,
addressing the questions of management? How can this be the
mobilisation of intellectual resource? Is it not a furtherance of
getting ideas out of the heads of bosses into the heads of labour?

It is important to make the poin here, and make it forcibly,
that the concept embodied in this chapter is not an espousal of
Japanese management and business methods, that debate is for
another forum, this article is about team management at all levels
and the communication system and methods upon which this
depends.

McWilliams (1990) has described the development of the
management ideal in the probation service and argues that a key
job of the manager, at every level, is to mobilise and put together
the intellectual resources of all staff. This implies a higher
expectation of all staff to use their intellectual resources in the
services of the organisation. For this to occur management must
be fertile ground for new ideas and management team
'group–think' cannot be allowed to cause ideas from below to be
cast as ridiculous or out of touch. At this point it may be worth

while considering the risks inherent in allowing a number of people room in which to tackle problems – the dangers of 'group–think'. Janis (1972) showed how important decisions can be seriously flawed when groups become over confident or when members come to assume the rightness of experts' opinions. Management of the type espoused by Matsuchita is not about a group being swept along by its own inertia, neither is it about leaderless teams, nor grass roots power. However, it is about management mobilising and putting together the intellectual resources of others in the organisation and that requires special attributes, special skills, and therefore training. It also raises the question: what is management? The word is used freely but often without agreed definition. When it is defined by its user it may be differently interpreted by the receiver. Easterby–Smith *et al.* made the distinction between management as a 'cadre' of people, and management as an activity. They observed that the title of manager is usually given to people in an organisation hierarchy who are at one or more levels above first line supervision. However, in the probation service everyone above main grade, except some individuals who bring special skills such as research and information, is usually deemed a manager. Easterby–Smith and his colleagues suggested that with 'the move towards flatter organisational structures which stress the importance of commitment, multi–skilled teams, minimum status and harmonisation, the traditional means of defining a manager is becoming increasingly problematic'. It can be argued that it has always been problematic within the probation service where staff have historically had some responsibility for the management of their resources. However, the service has moved, along with some other public sector organisations like the health service, against the tide by increasing its hierarchical structure and the number and proportions of persons deemed managers. Even so, the pyramid is still flat in probation when compared with other major criminal justice agencies such as the police and prison services, and still so after the relative size differentials have been taken into consideration.

With the increased emphasis on management has come increased expectations of management role, particularly in respect of corporate planning. Corporate planning is relatively new in the probation service. Elsewhere there is a vast literature on the subject. More than twenty years ago Steiner (1969) produced a bibliography of over 600 items. In probation services corporate planning is now seen as necessary for running the enterprise. But is this the right way to view it? As Ackoff (1970) observed:

Planning is predicated on the belief that the future can be

improved by active intervention now. Therefore it presupposes
some prediction of what is likely to come about if there is no
planned intervention. Such a prediction can be called a
reference projection. It attempts to specify what the future
states of the organisation being planned for will be if nothing
new is done (p.109).

This suggests that planning should not be about running the
business, but about aspirations, improvements and the attainment
of goals. In other words the improvement of output rather than
management of the *status quo*, and consequently, if maximum
improvement is to be achieved it demands the intellectual
resources of the total staff, not just the ideas of a small team of
individuals at the top however able they may be. This requires
that staff must know why the organisation is required to head in a
certain direction and the consequences of not doing so. Do all
probation staff at present know this? Did they know it at the time
the planning decisions were made? Did they contribute their
intellectual resources to those decisions? Were those decisions
informed by the particular knowledge and experiences of the total
staff? Or was it a process of ideas out of the heads of bosses into
the heads of labour? If the concept of putting together the product
of the intellectual resource is to be embraced, intellectual mobilisation must precede corporate planning; not the other way round.
Combined intellectual resource thus becomes a necessary prerequisite for planning if strategy is to be founded on the maximum
intellectual and experiential base.

Whilst support for the belief in the whole team (as distinct
from the management team and the workers) may challenge some
management as practiced, if not necessarily articulated in probation services, it does not challenge the concept of an objectives
driven organisation, provided the targets are informed and owned
by staff and are not as Matsuchita described 'ideas out of the
heads of bosses into the heads of labour'. That is a management
style which has hardly served Britain and the rest of Europe and
North America particularly well when compared with an aspect of
Japanese style espoused in this paper.

Clampitt (1991), in his inspirational book, pointed out in the
chapter entitled 'Communicating the Innovative Spirit' that with
a few exceptions, innovation has seldom been the product of a
few great minds or the reserve of managers:

> Tangled in the web of the 'big idea' theory of innovation is the
> belief that innovation can be done only by a select set of gifted
> individuals. Certainly some innovations, like genetic
> engineering or the silicon chip, would not have been possible

without the genius of a select few. But this does not mean that all innovations are the product of the gifted. Examples abound of the 'ordinary' individual coming up with some special and useful new innovation. Even the supposedly uninformed customer can sometimes be the source of useful innovation (p.77).

Clampitt continued 'Innovators may not necessarily be blessed with an apparent intellectual prowess. Rather, intellectual curiosity and drive are more important. Most great scientists have an IQ score of at least 120. Yet, after that point, there is little relationship between IQ and scientific success'. Quoting Beveridge (1980) Clampitt observed 'A scientist with an IQ of 130 is as likely to win a Nobel Prize as one with a score of 180', adding 'grades in school may not be a useful predictor of potential. Einstein and Darwin are two classic examples of poor students who clearly achieved some scientific fame. On the other hand, there are those who carried straight As at school but have never had a creative idea in their life'. This suggests that if the probation service relies either on its management to come up with the ideas or even to decide who should, the intellectual resource of the service will be going largely to waste, as it does in western manufacturing and service industry in abundance.

Implementation of the concept underlying this paper is dependent upon the style and ideology of managers and firm belief in the intellectual resource of all staff. However, it also places demands on training. There is a growing belief that business and training schools need to teach their students how to be managers and how to manage people rather than just teaching them *about* management (Bigelow, 1991). Compared with some organisations in commerce and industry, the probation service is particularly frugal with management training. Few staff receive instruction or training prior to taking up a more senior post and the training available following appointment to a senior position is often minimal and long after commencing the job when key decisions may already have had to have been made. Training is subject to different interpretations, from the development of conditioned response at one end of the continuum, to the acquisition of knowledge and theory at the other. The *Concise Oxford Dictionary* defines 'to train' as: 'To bring to a desired standard of efficiency by instruction and practice'. This is different to being taught about management, although it involves this. In the probation service many of the management concepts employed are self–taught or the result of one or several courses with little follow through or opportunity for feedback or correction of practice. Frequently, training is second hand since services have limited training budgets. One or perhaps several staff members undertake a course and are then expected to feed the wisdom back to the rest of the service. Senior probation officers are the first level of staff management. Their previous experience of managing people (unless they came to the service from another occupation) was as a main grade officer managing and enabling their clients. Is this adequate experience for managing other professionals? Yet the service expects that newly appointed seniors should be able to slip into the role with only a couple of weeks instruction and that often some time after taking up a post. In such a situation, for the newly appointed senior to set out deliberately to mobilise the intellectual resources of the team might be a very threatening exercise indeed and something to be avoided.

Delegation can be a fruitful route towards mobilising team resources. However, it also is a skill which requires training. Margerison and McCann (1990) point to Curtiss Peck of the National Consulting and Training Institution in the USA who views delegating as a six–step process.

Such a process avoids delegation by default and the offloading of responsibility. However, whilst the process as shown in Figure 9.1 is simple, the demands may be considerable. Both the selection and the training components are likely to involve the expenditure of resources but the competence which leads to confidence and trust enables the manager to build on and build up the intellectual resources of staff in the services of the organisation.

Staff management skills are not the only ones to be largely ignored by the service and its trainers. Few probation staff have been taught much criminology (although arguably they have been

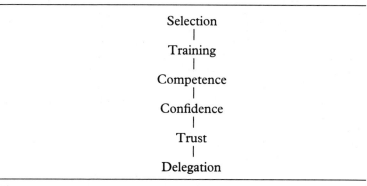

Figure 9.1

taught more than most police or prison officers), and initial course and in–service training teaches little about interview skills which should be among the more important tools. It seems not unreasonable to ask how management can effectively mobilise the intellectual resources of staff in working with criminals if there is a void in knowledge of criminology, interviewing skills and staff management techniques.

The overt manipulation of the probation service by government has been a recent phenomenon in the service's century long history and dates from the government's Financial Management Initiative (FMI) and the publication of the Home Office Statement of National Objectives and Priorities (SNOP) for the probation service in England and Wales (Home Office, 1984). The objectives, though largely imposed by the Home Office, seem in the main to have been accepted by service managers as not unreasonable and have undoubtedly pushed the service towards greater efficiency and effectiveness than it would otherwise have reached at this point in time. They have also caused it to look harder at its expectations of management. What has been absent is a sustained and common pattern of management throughout the service although HM Inspectorate of Probation has aimed at rectifying this through its programme of efficiency and effectiveness inspections. However, an unfortunate side effect of so called 'hard nosed management' is that ideas have tended to come from the top 'out of the heads of bosses into the heads of labour' and have taken the form of instructions, directives and complex processes as managers have struggled to formulate plans and ensure their implementation. This can choke communication systems, reduce the upward flow of ideas necessary for informing both the policy and its implementation and deny management the benefit of the intellectual resources of staff whose combined thinking power is very considerable indeed. The majority of probation staff (who are not managers) are at risk of being constrained by their role and having reduced opportunity to feed ideas to management and to innovate. The likelihood is that the gap between top management and field teams will widen. As the process continues, management will be able to draw upon less intellectual resource and finally only on its own, plus any think–tanks, specialist or individuals retained for particular purposes. Roles thus become compartmentalised and the organisation becomes the epitome of Matsuchita's model – a model which has failed the industrial West.

The management of sparsely populated regions provides an example of how the intellectual resources of staff have not been mobilised in order to tackle what is quite a serious justice issue.

Compared with most criminal justice agencies the probation
service has a commendable record for endeavouring to eliminate
inequality and injustice. However, attention to racism, sexism and
classism does not help people who are disadvantaged by the low
density of the population in which they reside. It has been noted
elsewhere that sparsity poses particular problems in relation to the
supervision of serious urban female offenders since there are often
insufficient at any one time or any one place to make groups
viable (HM Inspectorate of Probation, 1991). This phenomenon
applies also to both women and men living in rural districts but
on a very much larger scale. Most recent initiatives aimed at
developing community based facilities for offenders who might
otherwise be sent to prison have one thing in common – they are
suitable for well populated conurbations but unsuitable for
sparsely inhabited districts. Day centres, group programmes in
probation orders and groupwork requirements contained in community service national standards are all dependent upon a
generous sufficiency of suitable offenders within the defined
catchment area. In order that they can be managed economically
they require either centralised locations with adequate transport
links and/or high criminal activity within a small area. Whilst it is
possible to bus people to groups, this has considerable resource
implications. For a variety of social and other reasons the prison
population is composed largely of men from the cities and if they
were reduced the prison crisis would be alleviated. However, the
justice system does not – and if it does it should not – disregard
the existence of minorities for whom groups may be
impracticable, and consequently mete out differential justice. This
is neither just nor in the interests of the community.

Government is anxious that courts have available to them the
fullest range of sentencing options (Home Office, 1991). However, courts cannot have availability economically to day centres
and group facilities where the population is very thin. The task
facing services with large rural patches is therefore not how to
provide indentical justice to the densely populated urban areas
but how to provide equivalent justice to those areas. This challenge
brings with it the rider, how to be able to demonstrate efficiency
and effectiveness of the equivalent justice since once again, as
with the legislation, so also performance indicators and other
indices are geared to the urban context. Put another way, ideas
about the management of the probation service nationally have
developed with little influence from those staff whose intellectual
resources have been engaged in working with offenders in rural
locations. The management of offenders in rural locations has
suffered as a result of initiatives from the top, where the young

urban male crininal has been seen as the *main* problem – which he is – but treated as if he is the *only* problem - which he is not. It is the low population density over a big geographical area, rather than the small management structures which present the greatest difficulties, both in the development of provision and in evaluating the result of that provision.

The principle of evaluating the results of an endeavour against the resources consumed is not new; it has been around in the civil service and in industry in some form or another for at least half a century and has been used in commerce and the military for many hundreds of years. It is particularly interesting, therefore, that government and neo–government agencies, including the probation service, have only recently been required to demonstrate economic, efficient and effective use of resources in spite of the vast amounts of the nation's wealth which they have consumed jointly over the years. The surprising thing is that it has taken the probation service and the Home Office so long in coming to terms with the fact that some measure of performance should be attainable, would be beneficial to the service and is necessary both to it and to government which funds it. Or is that so surprising? The lack of scientific approach by successive governments has been offered time and time again as the major cause of Britain's economic and educational problems. Sir Dennis Rooke in his outgoing Presidential address to the British Association for the Advancement of Science criticised government's ignorance on scientific affairs, calling it 'abysmal' (Rooke, 1991). He had, of course, a point to make and a stance to take but even so it seems not unreasonable to suggest that if he was on the right lines in relation to matters which impinge directly on scientific research, how much greater may be the absence of a scientific approach in relation to other departments of government. There is indeed little sign that over many years the management of crime and criminals has been addressed in any way other than political expediency and ideological belief. This has fuelled the treatment *versus* punishment debate and the argument as to what effects could, and should, be measured. Whilst researchers both inside and outside government have demonstrated the effects and non–effects of policy, changes to policy which took account of the available evidence were slow to come and usually took second place to party political imperatives and short term financial expediency. Often evidence has been ignored and numerous examples of this are available, but the most important is probably the link between delinquency and the structure of poverty – inadequate education, poor housing, large family size, unemployment and lone teenage mothers, shown from the work of Farrington (1989) and supported by Graham (1989) in his review of the findings of other research. Both of these reports were published in Home Office Research Bulletins.

However, notwithstanding what has been said of past approaches, there has recently been a considerable change on the part of the Home Office towards the seeking of objective evidence as to the effectiveness of the probation service and this has found support, even if the methods chosen do not meet with universal approval. From the early 1980s onwards the Home Office has pushed the service towards developing systems which allow demonstration of its use of tax payers money. As was evident to probation officers this extended beyond simply showing value for money in the micro environment of the service itself, into the wider criminal justice system as government sought centre stage for the service to use it as a major tool in its efforts to tackle the financial, social, justice and political issues being forced upon it by the profligate use of imprisonment by British courts. The risks to the credibility of the probation service by this move were obvious at the time; if the service failed to influence the courts into using its products it could become the scapegoat of a failed justice system (Shaw, 1989). But how can the effectiveness of the service's efforts be measured when it is the courts and the courts alone which send people to prison? In the past the probation service has not been good at demonstrating results, even when some of these results were commendable (Shaw, 1990). This is starting to change but it is doubtful if it would have done so without the push from the Home Office and the demand for performance indicators. The regrettable thing is that indicators of services' and therefore of officers' performances, have been developed in almost complete isolation from those officers and the intellectual resources of the service and this has been a factor in the slow ownership of performance indicators. It has also led to important measures of efficiency which are evident to field officers, being absent from the formulae. For example a minority of cases, because of their characteristics and geographical location, consume an excessive amount of time.

May (1991), in his examination of change in the probation service, described the confusion as service managers employed performance indicators developed elsewhere and for other purposes as management tools. The confusion at team level is not surprising if staff have not been involved in *what* indicators demonstrate service, team and personal performance. First offenders provide an example. Nowadays, few would argue against some control over the number of trivial offenders made subject to probation or community service orders. However, the problem arises when the first offender has committed serious criminal acts, for instance multiple residential burglaries for which he is likely to be imprisoned. If the service is successful in persuading the court that its provisions are preferable to custody it will have achieved an objective of punishment in the community, nevertheless, it will also have increased its number of first offenders and, more importantly, since it will also have increased the total pool of people on probation, will have reduced the proportion on probation with previous convictions and previous custody.

Finch (1976) distinguished between 'management by objectives' where an individual is expected to strive towards the achievement of targets, and 'judgement by results' where the individual may be penalised if he or she tries but fails. If staff evaluation becomes based upon the achievement of objectives, which seems not unreasonable if the service is judged on the attainment of its objectives, it is important that staff are involved in the open setting of targets and an understanding of the factors involved if the system is not to deteriorate into judgement by results. The service as a whole is in the very same position as its individual staff members in respect of the expectations placed upon it as an agency charged with reducing the use of imprisonment. Consequently it is no longer sufficient for services simply to do good work with clients – it is sufficient only if they are able to demonstrate the effect of that work and that resources are being expended with the desired result and on the right clientele; in other words effectively and efficiently. These are complex issues requiring the intellectual resources of all staff in order that management can act on the maximum available knowledge, information and thought.

Efficiency and effectiveness were fundamental issues leading to Home Office production of SNOP and to the application of FMI to the probation service; yet they were largely ignored in over a third of local statements produced in response to SNOP (Lloyd, 1986). This was in spite of the evidence that for agencies to be funded to anything approaching the level they felt they required to provide adequate service, they would be expected to demonstrate value for money. In commercial organisations the principle index of performance is usually the generation of profit as the result of trading, although even this has to be gauged against the financial base of the company, its turnover, the potential market, the business environment and numerous other factors. An organisation such as a probation service does not have a clear index, indeed its very reason for existence may be different even in the minds of various members of its own staff and particularly so in the minds of those outside its boundaries be they in government, courts or the general public. In this respect it is perhaps worth remembering that not all observers are happy with the long term consequences as they see them, for instance, May (1991) argued that 'management by objectives in organisations with non–market criteria is highly problematic, while its uncritical adoption will almost certainly lead to dysfunctions in relation to its aims'. Accurate measurements of probation results are hard to describe and difficult to attain; indicators of performance on the other hand can be described and are more readily attainable. The risks, however, are that once produced they can become mythical 'statements of fact' and be used to support arguments for which they may be inappropriate, for instance, the application of urban targets and costs to rural communities. The confusion which exists in the service in relation to what demonstrates performance is partly because the intellectual resources of staff have not been brought to bear on the concept of demonstrating *team* achievement. Communication systems have not been developed to take account of 'ideas' from the intellectual resources of the service as a whole. The more information and instruction is pushed down through communication channels by management, the less space is available for information to come up – and instruction from the top takes precedence in most organisations, especially in meetings.

These are just some of the examples where developments in the service and implementation of government's objectives have been emerged upon without capitalising on the total available intellectual resources. As a result, decisions have been made on the basis of the intellectual resources of only a small segment of the organisation, that deemed by management as either its area of expertise or the job of a particular specialist. The reservoir of innovation has not been tapped and consequently ideas have come largely 'out of the heads of bosses into the heads of labour'.

Clampitt (1991) observed how many organisations tacitly communicate that innovation is the prerogative of one particular job. Ideas are thus rejected out of hand because they come from the wrong department, managers responding 'that's not really your concern'. Clampitt concluded 'Innovation is not the sole province of any one department or person, rather it should be a commitment of everyone in the organisation'. He went on to add:

> At county fairs across the land, blue ribbons are given for the best breads, jams ... The prizes do not go to those who follow the book; they go to those who dare to fail. After countless attempts and admitted failures, they succeed. Why? Persistence is part of it. But freedom – freedom to dream – is the critical factor. There is the freedom to change, to try

something new and different. There are no real boundaries. Unfortunately, tinkering is not encouraged in most organisations – red tape is. And no one is truly free if tangiled in the red tape. In the end, the result is paralysis; the red tape chokes off any change for the blue ribbon. But the red tape can be cut, procedures streamlined, and innovation can triumph. Churchill did it, and dedicated managers can as well.

The probation service is at the cross roads – it was always being told it was at a crossroads – but it really is this time. The double grip of Home Office direction and stronger management provides an opportunity for the establishment of clear objectives understood by all staff and a management philosophy and structure which encourages and enables the mobilising and putting together of the intellectual resources of all employees in the attainment of those objectives. Alternatively, and there are signs that this is happening already, it will increase the red tape and the bureaucracy, choke innovation and ensure that ideas come only 'out of the heads of bosses into the heads of labour'. Probation management, at all levels, will determine which route is followed and therefore the ultimate result – in Clampitt's terms – 'red tape or blue ribbon'. Matsuchita made the point more strongly: win or lose!

References

Ackoff, R.L. (1970) *A Concept of Corporate Planning*, New York, Wiley.

Ashworth, A. (1984) *Sentencing in the Crown Court*, University of Oxford: Centre for Criminological Research.

Beveridge, W.I.B. (1980) *Seeds of Discovery*, New York, Norton.

Bigelow, J.D. (1991) *Managerial Skills: Exploration in Practical Knowledge*, Newbury Park, Sage.

Clampitt, P.(1991) *Communicating for Managerial Effectiveness*, London, Sage.

Committee of Public Accounts (1990) Seventh Report, Home Office: Control and Management of the Probation Services in England and Wales, HMSO.

Easterby–Smith, M., Thorpe, R. and Lowe, A. (1991) *Management Research*, London, Sage.

Farrington, D. (1989) *The Origins of Crime: The Cambridge Study in Delinquent Development*, Home Office Research Bulletin No. 27, HMSO.

Finch, F. (1976) *A Concise Encyclopedia of Management Techniques*, Heinemann.

Graham, J. (1989) *Families, Parenting Skills and Delinquency*, Home Office Research Bulletin No. 26, HMSO.

Gummesson, E.(1988) *Qualitative Methods in Management Research* Bromley, Chartwell–Bratt.

Henderson, P.(1987) *Community Work and the Probation Service*, London, National Institute for Social Work.

HM Inspectorate of Probation (1990) *Probation Service Work in the Community*, HMSO.

HM Inspectorate of Probation (1991) *Probation Service Provision for Women Offenders*, HMSO.

Home Office (1962) *Report of the Department Committee on the Probation Service*, Cmnd. 1650. HMSO.

Home Office (1966) *Report on the Work of the Probation and After–Care Department 1962–1965*, Cmnd. 3107 HMSO

Home Office (1984) *Probation Service in England and Wales, Statement of National Objectives and Priorities*, HMSO.

Home Office (1990) *Supervision and Punishment in the Community*, Cmnd. 996, HMSO.

Home Office (1991) *Organising Supervision and Punishment in the Community*, HMSO.

Janis, I.L. (1972) *Victims of Group Think*, New York, Houghton Mifflin.

Lyoyd, C. (1986) *Response to SNOP*, Cambridge Institue of Criminology.

Margerison, C., and McCann, D. (1990) *Team Management*, London, Allen.

May, T. (1991) *Probation: Politics, Policy and Practice*, Buckingham, Open University Press.

McWilliams, W, (1990) 'Probation Practice and the Management Ideal', *Probation Journal*, June 1990.

Rooke, D. (1991) Outgoing Presidential Address to the British Association for the Advancement of Science, *Daily Telegraph*, 26.8.91.

Shaw, R. G. (1989) 'The Probation Service in a Flawed Justice System', *Probation Journal*, 36,1.

Shaw, R. G. (1990) 'Lies, Damned Lies and Statistics', *NASPO News*, 10,1.

Slater, D. (1989) 'Corridors of Power', in: J. Gubrium and D. Silverman (eds), *The Politics of Field Research*, London, Sage.

Steiner, G.A. (1969) *Top Management Planning*, New York, Macmillan.

Taylor, S.J. and Bogdan, R. (1984) *Introduction to Qualitative Research Methods*, New York, Wiley.

10 Partnerships in probation: setting the scene

Cedric Fullwood

If, for the purpose of the point I wish to make, we define the criminal justice system consisting of the police, prisons, prosecutors, sentencers, probation, and the clerks/courts administration, and then if we identify the main links between those groups and 'the voluntary sector', we arrive at an interesting picture. I am not here including a more general definition of community which would involve all these agencies on a larger scale. Perhaps —Table 10.1 is instructive.

Table 10.1 is of necessity partial and selective and there are many aspects of 'volunteers' and 'voluntary work' that could be slotted in alongside the criminal justice agencies referred to, but I have attempted to identify the main links and, in respect of the police, we are perhaps indulging in some licence with the concept of 'voluntary' by including paid special constables.

The two major areas of voluntary involvement in the criminal justice system from the above list is the large cadre of 'voluntary lay magistrates who deal with over 90 per cent of all court business, and the distinctive historical background and evolutionary experience of partnership in the probation service. In this chapter I am concentrating on the latter.

The history of the probation service reflects a sustained symbiotic relationship with the voluntary sector as well as partnerships with other statutory agencies, I would like to use two frameworks to highlight firstly the operational context of the probation service's work throughout the 20th century and, secondly, the structural context, which are those distinctive

Table 10.1

Criminal Justice System	Voluntary Sector
Police	Special Constables
Prison	Prison visitors/Boards of visitors
Crown Prosecution Service	Relationship with/ victims/witnesses
Sentencers	Lay magistracy
Clerks/Courts Administration	None
Probation	Historical roots in the voluntary sector and sustained partnership arrangements during the 20th century

features of the setting from which and in which the service works. During the post–Second World War years, the probation service began to build up its work in penal establishments, probation hostels and probation homes. Both of these developments had their roots in voluntary organisations, such as the National Association of Discharged Prisoners' Aid Society and the many religious organisations that provided residential facilities for individuals in need. It was not until as late as the 1960s that these two strands of work in the probation service took on a more profound statutory element. Another strand in the development of the probation service during the inter–war and post–war years, partly due to its religious and community base and also partly to the pioneer siting of probation offices in local communities, was the probation service's work in community conflict resolution. Even in the 1960s probation officers were carrying what were known as 'kindred social work' cases which included neighbours' quarrels and a range of social need which was partly shared with the local police station and, more recently, with social services departments. Finally, the 1970s saw the formal development of victim support – an indictment, if there ever was one, of the failure of the criminal justice system to respond to obvious personal and policy need. Despite the pioneering work of certain individuals and the enormous success of the National Association of Victim Support Schemes, as it was initially called, its operational background stems from a range of charitable and religious initiatives in the late 19th century. As now, there was a desperation in the penal system which was most officially articulated by the Gladstone Committee Report of 1895. This desperation focused on the large numbers of especially young offenders who were in adult prisons (and the humanitarian) as well as policy, concerns that this was wrong and should be changed. Taking the experience of conditional discharge from Massachusetts those original police court missionaries and the initial ideas behind probation orders attempted to divert, or use minimal intervention (to use the jargon of the late 20th century) to keep offenders in personal and social need out of prisons and occasionally out of courts. A range of help, including individual, family and social interventions was developed. This built on the traditions of Victorian philanthropy as well as modern casework developments, again drawn from the USA and pioneered in England by such organisations as the Charity Organisation Society.

In the inter–war years, the probation service could be seen engaging more with families, either in terms of matrimonial help or forms of religious counselling in family situations. On this latter point many urban probation areas had Catholic and Church of England probation officers specialising in work with individuals and families from their 'religious domain'. It must never be forgotten that the probation service, both through the commitment of individual probation officers and the general support of the service in general, played and continues to play an invaluable part in reaching out to the plight of victims. Bringing the historical picture up to date, we can see in the 1980s a distinctive development of the probation service's involvement in crime prevention, again in partnership with other statutory and voluntary agencies. The *raison d'être* for this involvement draws on the vast experience of probation areas and probation staff supervising thousands of offenders and working with their families in neighbourhoods, and writing thousands of reports and other assessments on offenders, their individual and social context. This vast wealth of experience enables the probation service to sit with others around the common community table to address issues of crime and breakdown in society and the social policy and personal strategies required to tackle them.

Turning now to the structural background to the development of the probation service, I think it is possible to identify certain distinctive features which characterise what initially was the development of the British Probation Service but after the Social Work Scotland Act of 1968 and the Black Committee Report in Northern Ireland is more properly identified as the English and Welsh Probation Service. Five aspects of this development have a bearing on our modern response to partnership.

Firstly, and already mentioned, are the voluntary roots going back into the 19th century of the development of the probation service. In fact, late into the 1930s the vast majority of probation officers were independent or voluntary.

Secondly is the probation committee, a body corporate consisting of mainly magistrates who are independent, both of central government and local authorities and who are charged with the responsibility of overseeing the policy and development of the local probation service. It was as the result of a Home Office Departmental Committee reporting in 1922 that probation committees were established (and on a much more structured basis from 1925 onwards). A concern for the early probation committees, through to the start of the Second World War, was the relationship between the more formal organisation of the probation service and the position of the voluntary organisations which had overseen its birth. In the early 1920s widespread criticisms were being voiced on the role of the major voluntary organisations. The tensions were between professional court social work and temperance propaganda. There was tension between the voluntary organisations requiring people to be of a particular religious and temperance persuasion, whereas probation officers wanted better training, qualifications, recognition, and a sound administrative base (whilst maintaining the religious and vocational commitment of the voluntary movement – known as having it both ways). It was not until the 1936 committee on 'Social Services in Courts of Summary Jurisdiction' that the nettle of the place of the voluntary societies in the probation system was grasped. That report insisted that probation should become a public service even though the religious and voluntary spirit in probation should not be lost.

The third feature of the structure of the probation service has been its legislative base from the 1907 Probation of Offenders Act, through the major seminal legislation of the 1948 Criminal Justice Act and some would say encapsulated in yet another major piece of legislation, the 1991 Criminal Justice Act. This legislative base which has been sustained periodically throughout almost every decade of this century, gives the probation service in England and Wales a distinctive character and profile.

Fourthly, another feature in the structure of the probation service has been its relationship with the criminal justice system as a whole, even though that phrase has a later derivation. We should never forget the scale on which probation supervision was used in the 1930s, when as many as 35% of all court disposals were probation based – something which makes our current 10% to 15% look like a real reduction. A complex message lies behind these bare statistics, in that in the early part of the century it was considered morally good and professionally correct treatment to intervene early in criminal careers. This has changed over recent years, and now the probation service is concentrating on more difficult and demanding offenders at a later stage in their criminal careers, although prospects of a further discussion document from the government on the causes of criminality might return us to our original base. The sustained relevance, almost centrality of the probation service in the criminal justice system is a distinctive feature that must be borne in mind in discussions regarding partnership with the voluntary and private sector, as well as other statutory agencies. The features of this relationship within the criminal justice system have changed significantly over time. An experienced stipendiary magistrate in the early part of this century used to refer to probation officers as the 'scavengers' of the court, tiptoeing in to collect drunken offenders and prostitutes to try and help rehabilitate them. The 1948 Criminal Justice Act and later reports on the probation service underscored probation officers as the 'servant of the court' – something that is still referred to even though the wearing of hats by women officers and formal dark suits and striped trousers by male officers in Crown Courts has disappeared. It is in the 1980s that the probation service's relevance within the criminal justice system could be characterised by the word 'partner'. These developments, its legislative base and its probation committee structure gives the probation service a unique position in any partnership with others dealing with offenders in relationship to courts, penal establishments, as well as its position within the community. These distinctive characteristics must be borne in mind in partnership work.

The fifth and final feature of the structure of the probation service to highlight is the development since 1960 of 'Care Trusts'. During the 1960s, policy, as well as legislative developments, were placing more and more responsibilities on the probation service. Its working relationship with central government for resourcing, as well as policy direction, became more and more complex and, in some respects, long term. Probation staff up and down the country began to seek for alternative methods of taking initiatives, acquiring alternative resources for innovative projects and engaging the wider community in the management of these locally based projects. The Selcare Trust, which is now based in Greater Manchester but had its origins in 1969 in South–East Lancashire, was one of the pioneering bodies in this respect. The charitable trust status, and then later the acquisition of housing association status, made this and other care trusts a quiet but potent force in the development of facilities within the community and also the promotion of wider partnership between the judiciary, local authority and commercial and voluntary networks in the local area.

If the above developments are not enough the review, monitoring and policy changes that we have seen throughout the 1980s confirm the pace of change which will take us to the turn of the century. It is for others to write the history of criminal justice and the role of statutory and voluntary agencies in dealing with offenders in the 1980s. However, some of the features of such a history will highlight: the questioning and heart searching in relation to the role of the local authorities and the public sector generally; the emphasis on private sector models of organising services; and the search for economy, efficiency and effectiveness at every turn. In the wider government field this came to a head with major legislative developments, such as the National Health Service and Community Care Act and the related emphasis on purchaser/provider splits. A variety of efficiency scrutinies within government, overseen in the first part of the decade by one of the Directors of Marks and Spencer (Lord Rayner), brought a speed and focus and, at times, a critical and threatening viewpoint to bear. In respect of the voluntary sector this was articulated in the Efficiency Scrutiny of Government Funding of the Voluntary Sector published in 1990 and the government action response to it published in 1991 *Profiting from Partnership: The Implementation Process*. To the extent that services and facilities for offenders involve the Department of the Environment, especially from a housing perspective, the Department of Health and Social Security, as well as the Department of Employment, this review process and the principles enunciated was critical. However, the Home Office instituted in 1990 its own review on 'Partnership in Dealing with Offenders in the Community' which was a discussion paper aimed at complementing the White Paper on Crime, Justice, and Protecting the Public, as well as the Green Paper on 'Supervision and Punishment in the Community: A Framework for Action'. This discussion paper led to one of the most substantial consultations between the probation service and voluntary agencies and community groups ever seen since the 1930s. We must not underestimate the scale and significance of that debate and consultation process.

The Home office discussion paper identifies the purpose of partnership in the context of the White and Green Papers on punishment in the community as giving increasing support for efforts to provide effective community based penalties for offenders. I suggest, drawing on the historical and professional developments referred to earlier in this chapter, that real partnership should be tackling expanded aims which should include:

- a fairer and more effective criminal justice system including attending to the plight of victims in general and also to black defendants in particular

- constructive facilities and programmes which will re–establish and rehabilitate offenders in working communities

- revitalise the probation service's commitment to civil work and extend this to the needs of children in domestic and family breakdown within our criminal and penal responsibilities.

The complexity of working with offenders in their individual, family and social context, is difficult enough, but working in partnership with other agencies and other groups, whilst necessary, is even more complicated. It might be helpful to identify four key themes in taking partnership forward:

1. Policies should be designed to enhance the work of the probation service and not used as a means of obtaining services 'on the cheap' or simply in pursuit of a doctrinaire determination to achieve a mixed economy.

2. There should be maximum flexibility for probation areas to reach local agreements about work to be undertaken by other agencies, and it would be far better to utilise existing probation committee structures and inter–agency groups to promote the partnership concept in practice, rather than establishing new committees or structures. The service should provide the leadership.

3. There should be adequate *new* finance available to ensure that such work is competently performed.

4. Administrative arrangements, including monitoring and accountability, should be as simple as possible to ensure the cooperation and active support of the independent sector, especially local organisations and groups.

A theme in public policy generally in the 1980s has been the role of the private sector and this has been introduced by the Home Office in relation to dealing with offenders in the community. I must stress that the notion of competitive tendering in respect of services to offenders in the criminal justice system is unacceptable and sits uneasily, to put it mildly, with the notion of partnership. The private sector has some, but nevertheless limited, roles in partnership arrangements. This is not to diminish the major achievements to date, such as in Greater Manchester Probation Service where a quarter of a million pounds was provided by British Telecom to fund a pre–employment training centre which radically approached job placement opportunities for probationers and others on supervision. Rather the private sector is limited in respect of the range of activities and developments it can participate in, never mind take responsibility for, under the heading of dealing with offenders in the community.

The modern probation service is dealing with more difficult offenders and more complex social problems. Our experience convinces us that effective responses to both offenders and crime, as well as family breakdown, is an integrated one: a wholesome, constructive process which combines rehabilitation and control; it would be a dangerously flawed professional, as well as policy development to separate out core control elements from help and facilities which are critical to support and supervision programmes.

Taking stock of partnership developments at the beginning of the 1990s leaves the unwitting commentator in danger of being too influenced by the immediate past decade with its distinctive political approach to the delivery of public services and the role and responsibilities of the individual *vis-à-vis* the community/state. This is why I have considered it so important in reviewing these developments and considering the future to set the debate in the context of the history of the probation service and the major milestones and staging posts in our development. We will draw more strength from consideration of the essential truths that lie behind those development than concentrating on the more ephemeral changes, as they will come to be seen, of the past few years. Nevertheless, the strength of the probation service is not its backward looking or reactionary stance, but, as the Audit Commission report commended, its imaginative, flexible and pioneering approach to taking new initiatives in the face of the continuing challenges that lie ahead.

Let me conclude by reflecting on the partnership concept from three different perspectives: relationships, resourcing and management. Firstly, in terms of relationships the development of partnerships will require a fundamental shift from central to local control. The history of developments with the voluntary sector have seen a bias towards central intervention by the State, either directly or via national voluntary organisations. There will continue to be a need for central policy and a national strategic overview in which the robust and pioneering contribution of the national voluntary societies should go from strength to strength. However, the real delivery of services to critical social problems and individuals in need is at local level. Probation committees forming alliances with other statutory and voluntary agencies and community groups locally must have more responsibility for tackling these problems and being held to account. Within this context of relationships the probation service itself has to be mature enough to realise that it alone is not the repository of all wisdom, knowledge and skill in relation to dealing with offenders and family breakdown in communities. Its ability to learn from other experiences, to cede power and to learn from the insights of others about the limitations of the probation organisations, will put it in an immeasurably more confident and healthy position.

Secondly, in relation to resourcing, we must acknowledge the incredible amount of resources poured into the criminal justice system over the past ten or twenty years. It behoves us all to pool those finite resources, rather than garner them in darkened bunkers, worried about the predatory activities of others. But more importantly, our major resource is one of ideas and we must all promote radical responses to our penal and criminal justice crises.

Thirdly, is the challenge for management in the probation service, as well for the voluntary sector. Other contributors to this book give attention to some of the management implications of developments in the partnership field, whether to do with the purchaser/provider split if this is sustained over the next five to ten years, or the underlying need for coherent local strategies, properly informed and monitored. New roles and responsibilities need to be developed, both at the Headquarters of probation areas and its committee structure, as well as in the tasks required by middle managers and team leaders. New skills for delivering services and providing facilities need to be integrated into the work of the modern day probation service. The local team/area manager needs to be able to put together a complex structure of services and facilities which draw on the strengths of other providers, alongside the specific contribution of probation teams. The training and organisational implications are profound, but ones I think many probation areas are already facing with vigour and vision.

The 1936 report on the provision of Social Services in Magistrates' Courts heralded the demise of the voluntary sector role in the probation service of the 1930s and 1940s which was to emerge after the Second World War under the umbrella provisions of the 1948 Criminal Justice Act. That report concluded that a splendid chapter in English social history was at an end. Dare we, in these troubled times, when current social policies appear as rice paper in response to the deluge of appalling problems individuals and families face, dare we speak of a new splendid chapter in English social history opening up? If we could and if we had the vision, that would indeed be a testimony to our predecessors who met and worked a hundred years ago, with challenges not dissimilar to those we face at the end of this century. At the beginning of this chapter, I used the phrase 'symbiotic'. If this is a relevant biological term to translate to probation work, we should remember that in such relationships the association is advantageous to both organisms.

11   Partnerships: the Northern Ireland dimension

Breidge Gadd

Introduction

Northern Ireland, with its separate legislative and governing body between 1921 and 1971 developed its personal social services with quite a different administrative structure from the rest of the UK. The probation service, although similar in philosophy, legislation and practice to the rest of the UK, from 1950 onwards became part of the Civil Service, which was then the Ministry of Home Affairs and after direct rule in 1972 the Northern Ireland Office. Although neither Seebohm nor Kilbrandon included Northern Ireland in their remit the 1960s wind of change did not bypass Northern Ireland and in 1976 a government inter-departmental review group was established under the chairmanship of Sir Harold Black, with terms of reference which included the review of children and Young Persons legislation and also to consider the future administration of the probation service. The Black Report, as it is popularly referred to, reported in 1979 and made recommendations regarding the treatment of juvenile offenders. The recommendations for the development of the probation service were straightforward and in terms of its farsightedness the *raison d'être* is worth quoting as follows:

> 7.4   We consider that the probation service should remain a separate service specialising in dealing with offenders and serving the criminal courts. The service should continue to be responsible for the development and the oversight of all non–custodial disposals where supervision in different degrees

is envisaged. It should have responsibility for any day attendance or residential centres. The service should also be the main source of social information for the criminal courts. Its aim should be to make the non custodial disposals as effective as custody in preventing reoffending, at least for the period during which offenders are under supervision.

7.5   The service is at present administered directly by the Northern Ireland Office and from an administrative point of view this may well be satisfactory. However, if the service is to enjoy fully the confidence of the community, which will be essential if it is to carry out its work successfully, we consider that this can be better achieved if the community participates directly in the management of the service. We recommend therefore that the probation service be administered by a Board drawn from a wide spectrum of the community in Northern Ireland. This Board will be responsible for the administration and policy management of the probation service in its expanded role.

7.6   The main thrust of the service's activities as we see it will be the provision of a specialist service to the courts and involvement with the community in the management of the offender.

The Probation Board

In 1982 an order in Council, the legal mechanism in Westminster for introducing legislation specific to Northern Ireland, passed the Probation Board (Northern Ireland) Order 1982. Thus it was that in 1982 a new organisation was created and in December of the same year the first Probation Board took up post. To establish the first Board a wide ranging number of relevant bodies were approached by the Northern Ireland Office and asked to submit names of members who might be interested in serving on the Board. The first Board members were then selected from the voluntary sector, the CBI, trades unions, local councillors, the law society, retired prison service administrators, the youth service, the lay juvenile magistrate court and the board of prison visitors. Readers familiar with probation committees composed largely of magistrates will be interested to hear that apart from the juvenile court lay magistrate, the stipendiary magistrate nor judiciary have ever been part of the Northern Ireland Probation Board. The Board, therefore, provides a service to the courts and to prisons but staff are not employed by the courts.

The Black Report made two further recommendations which

were not included in the legislation. The first was that a written code of conduct should be drawn up for the probation service in consultation with the courts to ensure that the courts, the public, the probation officer and offender are all familiar with the minimum expectations and requirements of the particular form of supervision imposed by the courts – the precursor of our present day standards of practice. The second recommendation was that the Board should be responsible for the custodial unit for juveniles, but again, was not implemented.

The legislative functions of the Board outlined in the Probation Board Order (1980) were articulated as follows:

4 1 (a)　secure the maintenance of an adequate and efficient probation service;

(b)　secure that arrangements are made for persons to perform work under community service orders;

(c)　provide such probation officers and other staff as the Secretary of State considers necessary to perform social welfare duties in prisons and young offender centres and;

(d)　undertake such other duties as may be prescribed.

2(a)　provide and maintain probation hostels and other establishments for use in connection with the supervision and assistance of offenders;

(b)　provide and maintain bail hostels;

(c)　make and give effect to schemes for the supervision and assistance of offenders and the prevention of crime;

(d)　enter into arrangements with voluntary organisations or any other persons (including government departments and public bodies) whereby those organisations or persons undertake, on such terms (including terms as to payment by the Board to those organisations or persons) as may be specified in the arrangement;

(i)　the provision and maintenance of such hostels and other establishments as are mentioned in sub–paragraphs (a) and (b);

(ii)　to give effect to such schemes as are mentioned in sub-paragraph (c)(p.3).

Before commenting on how the Board has operated during the past decade, let me first identify the differences between the Northern Ireland probation service and the service in England and Wales. It seems to me that there are two significant differences. Firstly, the probation service in Northern Ireland apart from supervising domestic 'lifers' does not carry any statutory responsibility for throughcare, nor is there any provision for supervised parole. Apart from life sentence prisoners released on supervised or unsupervised licence, all prisoners automatically receive half remission of sentences. Our work, therefore, in prisons with released prisoners and with prisoners' families is offered as a service to be accepted or rejected according to its perceived usefulness.

The second major difference is that in Northern Ireland the probation service does not engage in any civil work. Since the late 1970s the probation service and social services agreed that divorce court welfare, adoption and guardian ad litem work, should be the responsibility of social services departments which is now enshrined in law. Therefore, the probation service in Northern Ireland is firmly based in service provision to all the criminal courts regarding reports and community supervision, but works with prisoners and their families largely on a voluntary basis.

Board effectiveness

Before looking in detail at the question of partnership it might be worth commenting on the first ten years experience of a community based Board. Board members including the chairman and deputy chairman are appointed by the Secretary of State for a three year term and only in exceptional circumstances serve for more than two terms. Board membership therefore changes every three years, which requires a commitment to ongoing induction and training for new members. This can be a time–consuming process, but more importantly begs the question of the appropriate length of time for lay persons appointed to public office to serve. Furthermore, how long does it take, and what are the necessary ingredients in terms of qualities, values and experience to make an individual capable of becoming the employer of a professional service staffed with professionally qualified officers whose job is largely prescribed by legislation?

The 1980s and in particular the Thatcher years seemed to believe that any dissolution of the power of the public professional i.e. lawyer, social worker, medical practitioner, was a good thing in itself. The same period, however also saw the growth of the notion of equality of opportunity, of open, objective and fair recruitment and appointment to jobs in both the public and private sector in order to reduce prejudice or the fear of prejudice. It is therefore somewhat ironic that public boards, set up quite legitimately and positively to curb professional power, and indeed to ensure accountability, are selected and appointed using a hidden and secretive process. It is in the area of the selection of Board members that certain issues must be addressed: What should be the process of selection of members of the public to oversee professional services? What are the qualities we should be looking for? What previous experience should we be looking for?

Performing such a complex role successfully requires knowledge of organisations, management, the role and function of a Board and its relationships with its chief executive. Board membership also requires wisdom and self–confidence in order on the one hand to influence, challenge, shape and to monitor policy, but on the other hand to remain outside the minutiae of management. It also, in the case of the probation service, requires in the individual appointed, a sense of values and attitudes which largely are in support of the aims and purposes of the probation service. One could, of course, argue that magistrates or in the case of the personal social service, the local councillor, do not necessarily possess the above–mentioned qualities. Indeed, I am sure that this is too often the case, although magistrates do have an expertise in the criminal courts and an understanding of the role of the probations service in the courts and councillors are elected to office and therefore represent the local community, although they may not especially have experience or interests which equip them in the art of Board membership. It does seem critical, however, whether for probation committees in England and Wales or for the Board in Northern Ireland, that much more thought than was previously the case is given to the job specification, the personnel specification, the length of time of appointment and then to the selection and training of Board or committee members who agree to assume responsibility as the employers of the probation service. This is particularly important with the advent of cash limits and the enhanced policy and monitoring role for committees currently being advocated by the Home Office in England and Wales.

Highlighting the need for attention to be given to the area of selection of Board Members does not in any way negate the notion of a community based Board representing the major stakeholders or customers of the probation service. The probation service in Northern Ireland has benefited greatly from having community representatives as employers of the service. A good Board or committee can act as a buffer between the service and government. Members from different elements within the community can use their contacts and influence in enhancing external relations but most importantly of all, the community has an investment in and a sense of ownership in the service. In

Northern Ireland, where communities both catholic and protestant feel alienated, acceptance of the probation service is a critical factor. In the more ordered society of England and Wales it may not be so essential. However when one looks at some of the ethnic minority communities in some of the urban developments, problems for the probation service caused by a lack of ownership and distance from the community may also be a greater problem than is presently realised.

Partnership

As well as establishing a community based Board the Northern Ireland Order in 1982 empowered the Board to purchase or to grant aid to the private or voluntary sector. The first Board, in its corporate plan, outlined its commitment to working in partnership with the community and voluntary sector as outlined in its mission statement: to be recognised as an organisation which helps local communities acknowledge the causes and consequences of crime and develop strategies for dealing with them; to be an organisation committed to supporting and encouraging initiatives in the prevention of offending demonstrated by resourcing a significant number of schemes designed to that end.

Now, in 1992, approximately one–sixth of the annual budget is paid to community voluntary organisations. Most of the money is used to purchase services and a smaller amount is used to support new initiatives which the probation service considers are worth funding. In broad terms the projects funded by the Probation Board in Northern Ireland can be divided into the following categories:

1. Accommodation – all the specialist hostel facilities for offenders in Northern Ireland are provided by the voluntary sector.

2. Prisoner family services – these range from cafés or canteens for families in visitors' waiting areas in prison to a joint probation/voluntary organisation drop-in centre with a whole range of facilities available, such as benefits advice and baby sitting.

3. Employment services – the Board in partnership with the Training and Employment Agency funds specialist workshops for offenders. Additionally the probation service and two of the main voluntary specialist offender agencies have combined to form a separate company which is a managing agency specialising in job training programmes

for ex–offenders and clients considered to be at risk.

4. Fourth condition/specified activity programmes – range
    from a nineteen day residential order for adult offenders to
    intermediate treatment type projects in the community,
    run largely by local community groups which can be used
    as a fourth condition/specified activity programme as part
    of a probation order. Moreover, crime prevention and
    other grants can be given either for specific local crime
    prevention schemes or to support a non–statutory
    organisation providing a scheme useful to offenders, such
    as a debt counselling agency.

It is interesting that the government Blue paper discussion
document 'Organising Supervision and Punishment in the
Community', published during 1991, questions whether in
England and Wales the voluntary sector should run programmes
which address offending behaviour. In Northern Ireland our
experience has shown that this artificial dichotomy, between
statutory and voluntary, does not exist. Indeed, community
workers, in some cases the parents of young offenders themselves,
are particularly adroit at helping the offender to face up to and
take responsibility for his or her actions. One could go on to say
that it is because of the relevance and effectiveness of the
approach that Northern Ireland Probation Board members and
staff continue to be committed to the notion of partnership
between community and probation service, recognising the
possibilities of behaviour change in young offenders especially
when local people are involved.

Experience has also taught us over the past ten years to be
careful about definitions. What precisely do we mean by the term
'voluntary organisation'? There are in Northern Ireland, as there
are in England and Wales, non–governmental and non–statutory
public bodies, for example NACRO, who do an excellent job in
providing services but who are not essentially any more a part of
the local community than the probation service or any other
statutory organisation. The benefit of using such voluntary
organisations in the supervision of sometimes difficult offenders is
that they can provide high quality, innovative facilities, more
effectively and cheaper than the statutory organisation. They also
have the major advantage of offering choice and a change of
culture to the customer. However, purchasing services in this area
of provision for offenders while good for the offender raises its
own set of problems for the voluntary organisations. The disadvantages can often be a limited budget and big demands on the

voluntary sector. In order to be constructive both statutory and voluntary organisations need to have clarity of objective, clarity of financial support and agreed performance indicators and measurements. Community groups which evolve or are set up to deal with specific problems of crime or offenders do not, by their existence, reduce the workload of the probation officer; in some instances quite the reverse. The pay–off is that a scheme evolving from the community which tackles a local problem of crime is likely to be much more successful than one imposed from outside by a statutory agency. The workload emphasis is different rather than reduced. Consequently, in conclusion, it may be helpful to point out some of the partnership issues with the community we are beginning to address in Northern Ireland which may be of benefit to England and Wales.

1. Partnership is not an equal sharing of responsibility on a fifty-fifty basis; the statutory agency must always carry the major responsibility and constant clarification of roles, at all levels, is necessary as well as clear lines of accountability.

2. The question of who initiates schemes and projects can become critical and tensions can arise when a community group or voluntary organisation wants to run a project which the probation service considers is not required.

3. Northern Ireland still operates a system of grant aid although it is moving towards competitive tendering. This in itself raises a series of new dilemmas. Do we wish to set hard pressed voluntary groups against each other in order to pare costs to a minimum, especially when the client group to be worked with is certainly difficult and occasionally dangerous?

4. Although the concept of the private market led approach is attractive, there is no rush in Northern Ireland of private profit–making organisations anxious to run hostels for difficult offenders.

5. In management resource terms we are still trying to find the right formula, ranging from a specialist assistant chief probation officer for community development, to community partnership as an integral part of a generalist ACPOs workload. Certainly extra resources and training are needed in the research and administration departments.

In the last analysis, there is much to think about if the probation service in England and Wales is about to launch into the partnerships business.

References

Northern Ireland Office (1979) 'Legislation and Services for Children and Young Persons in Northern Ireland' The Black Report,
HM Government Probation Board: Northern Ireland (1980) HMSO.

12 Purchasing and providing services for offenders: lessons from America

Mary Fielder

There is nothing new in the idea of statutory agencies acquiring services by contract with others. In recent years local authorities have increasingly used this method in preference to direct provision, and the probation service is accustomed to the process of competitive tendering of contracts for building work and other technical and manual services. Since 1984 metropolitan areas are no longer tied to local authorities for arranging their personnel, financial, legal and building functions. Whilst most metropolitan areas have taken such functions in–house, a number are already buying–in services; Shire counties are now considering the benefits of such independence. The Audit Commission Occasional Paper (1991) reported that there were instances where probation committees were being overcharged by local authorities for central services because it was known that costs charged to the service are 80% refunded by the government. With cash limits, probation committees will be increasingly concerned to review expenditure and identify where savings may be achieved by alternative arrangements.

However, in the next decade probation managers will be faced with quite new considerations in purchasing service contracts. It is suggested that direct services to offenders may be provided by other agencies with probation officers becoming the broker of such resources. At a limited level such arrangements already exist with offender accommodation being largely provided by voluntary organisations and the Northern Ireland Probation Board already has grant aiding powers, but there is encouragement for all probation services to expand contract provisions more widely. The Home Office paper on Partnership in Supervising Offenders in the Community invited a response on a range of such proposals and the Criminal Justice Act 1991 introduces an enabling power for probation committees in England and Wales to grant aid to encourage joint development with the voluntary and independent sector. The Audit Commission has commented that the Service will need additional management skills to establish contract arrangements.

A future probation service with its role in supervision restricted to assessment and the enforcement of court orders, whilst others engage in tackling the personal and social problems of offenders, is not an attractive proposition for either managers or practitioners. Uneasy glances are cast in the direction of social services departments. A key objective in the purchaser/provider split introduced by the NHS and Community Care Act of 1989 is to transform social service authorities into enabling agencies with responsibility to make maximum possible use of private and voluntary providers, and thus increase the available range of options and widen consumer choice. However, the major imperative for the new community care arrangements was to reduce spending on social care. Could the same principle be applied to the probation service once cash limits are effected, and what might be the results?

To reduce the likelihood of unplanned or unintended consequences of change, the key objectives for reform need to be identified. The changes planned in the way in which social care is delivered, or initially advised by the inquiry and subsequent report of the committee chaired by Sir Roy Griffiths, were identified in the White Paper 'Caring for People'. Successful implementation of major change requires a planned strategy, and careful management during the planning and transitional phase. The series of implementation documents prepared by the Department of Health and advisory reports of the Social Services' Inspectorate have provided detailed guidance to social service authorities in drawing up their community care plans. It has also been recognised that monitoring and evaluation will be needed to measure outcome and performance achievement. No comparable thought or planning has gone into the delivery of effective supervision to offenders in the community. There is no equivalent of the Griffith's review of what services are required to meet the risks and needs posed in supervising offenders in the community. There has been no assessment of how, and by whom, the required services should be delivered, and no advice to probation managers on developing a strategy to encompass an enhanced use of contract provision. In the absence of any apparent national strategy, are probation managers faced with unique problems or unique opportunities?

Developing contracts for services is not the same thing as grant aiding, albeit the latter may include some specified requirements as to the nature and size of service which the funder requires the providing agent to deliver. The Voluntary Aftercare Grant Scheme, administered by the Home Office, is a typical example of grant aiding with strings, and to the voluntary organisations involved is experienced as a contractual arrangement. True contracts, however, impose legal obligations and whilst there may be varying degrees of detail in the content about the service to be provided, contracts will need to specify certain minimum terms. There are numerous publications on the subject of contracts between statutory agencies and voluntary organisations, which have appeared in the wake of community care planning. A thoughtful and helpful introduction being 'Contracts for Social Care: The Local Authority View' published by the Association of Metropolitan Authorities. 'Getting Ready for Contracts: a Guide for Voluntary Organisations', in the Contract Culture Series has a useful essential reading list.

The scope for developing a purchaser/provider split in the arrangements for the supervision of offenders raises considerations of a quite different order. How far can the responsibility for court ordered restrictive penalties be delegated to agencies not directly accountable to publicly appointed or elected authorities? Equally importantly, would voluntary organisations be prepared to enter such contracts? The private sector is unlikely to be faced with the same philosophical dilemmas, but probation managers, staff and their unions, will have strong reservations about buying services from those whose business is profit. What experience has there been to advise the decisions which must soon be taken? The country which has contracted offender services more widely than any other is the United States. Whilst the differences in the administration of justice, to say nothing of culture, do not make for easy direct comparison, there is much that is directly relevant in the American experience.

The extent to which American probation organisations contract with private and voluntary agencies for the delivery of services is highly variable. However, the nature of the services purchased tends to follow a similar pattern, and includes principally:

- urinalysis and substance abuse treatment
- residential provision
- electronic monitoring
- community service
- bail information, discontinuance and diversion programmes
- employment training and placement
- support and technical services

The use of purchased services in the United States is more often the result of political pressure or pragmatic considerations than a planned review of needs and options. Outside the federal system, each probation service is separately administered at state or county level, and thus not immune from the prevailing political and economic environment. The factors relevant in decisions to buy services are phrased in different language and more bluntly expressed than might be expected in the UK, strike a familiar chord, and fall under three main headings which are political, economic and opportunistic.

Political

Any growth in the public sector in the United States is deemed to be electorally unpopular. As a result, both state officials and chief officers of probation are acutely aware that elected representatives will resist any increase in the salaries budget of state departments and new monies for development can best be achieved through service contracts. Political pressure can also work in the opposite direction. When services are provided by a large number of independent organisations, each with a political representative who can be canvassed for support when the department's budget is under review by the state government, there is a better chance that resources can be retained.

Economic

Contract services are deemed to be both more economic and more efficient than directly provided services. In revenue terms, the savings are generally estimated to be in the region of 20 to 30 %. Whilst competitive tendering has helped to achieve greater economy, it is also acknowledged that the lower salaries paid by the independent sector are a significant factor. Capital cost savings are achieved as the provider is normally responsible for all plant, equipment and setting up finance.

Opportunistic

With a healthy and competitive independent sector offering a range of specialised facilities, there is little justification for the probation service to duplicate that provision. The existence of such a rich pool of privately managed facilities is both a cause and effect of the American system. The absence of a National Health Service, and the greater reliance on personal and company insurance schemes, has encouraged the growth of private treatment and counselling services. Services initially developed to meet the demand from private buyers have increasingly marketed their facilities to the public sector under contract arrangements.

Another principle advantage of contract provision is deemed to be the ability to achieve change more quickly than would be possible in a public sector department making direct provision. A classic example is perhaps the Department of Youth Services in Massachusetts. In order to overcome the resistance to change on the part of departmental staff and their unions, the then Commissioner for Youth Services turned to the independent sector to develop the new community homes which were essential to replace the former juvenile training schools. Not only is it held that the non–statutory sector can provide new facilities more quickly, but the purchaser can also transfer contracts if the service provided does not meet expectations. Whilst most of these factors are, or may become, as relevant in the UK as the US, they have to be seen in the context of the probation task. Whilst there are presently significant differences, if a contract culture and other related changes were to develop then these differences are likely to diminish.

In the absence of specific pre–entry training, probation officers in the US do not see themselves as equipped to provide skilled counselling on an individual or group basis. Such problems as sexual deviancy, or family disfunctioning, are deemed to be the province of specialists whose services have to be bought-in. Probation officers see themselves primarily as law enforcers, a position which has emerged from a number of experiences. The 'nothing works' research of the 1970s had a profound influence in the US. If treatment was ineffective, other performance indicators, i.e. compliance, had to be established with probation as a sentence in its own right, and a tendency to add on numerous other conditions, such as restitution, fees, and substance abuse monitoring, probation staff have considerable responsibility for organising and administering non–social work tasks. Whilst some probation managers are now strongly advocating a return to social work principles, others are anxious to ensure that staff focus on their primary tasks, and are not confused or diverted by a dual responsibility of acting as counsellor. How successful has the American experience been? What are the pitfalls in the arrangements, and what are the relevant considerations for probations managers in this country?

Some of the principle advantages quoted by those advocating contracting with independent and voluntary organisations, are those of innovation and flexibility, such agencies' roots in, and support from, local communities, and the greater choice offered to users when services are not in the hands of a single provider. Such qualities have high value, and characterise the work of many voluntary groups large and small. They have developed in organisations which are usually engaged in a range of other tasks, advocacy, campaigning, education, community work and self–help projects. The experience in North America would suggest that if voluntary organisations are increasingly dependent on contract funding, these other activities, and thus their uniquely independent role, are under threat. For both purchaser and provider, the American experience suggests that the pitfalls are very real and some of the disadvantages from a purchaser point of view are as follows:

1. Public contracts favour large organisations. Whilst many departments place contracts with a large number of organisations, the majority tend to go to a handful of better resourced agencies. Small voluntary groups lack the administrative skills and infrastructure to tender for contracts, or to meet the statistical and monitoring returns required by the purchaser.

2. Independent providers can and do develop into monopolies. Where the public sector is no longer delivering a particular service, the independent agency thus becomes the single provider, with all the obvious attendant problems for the purchaser.

3. Switching resources from one provider to another is not an easy task, and a disruption in services to the user is difficult to avoid. It can also prove difficult to withdraw funding from the independent sector, which may have much political support and utilise that effectively in lobbying to retain resources.

4. Where provision is made privately, there is no guarantee of permanence and if a project is insufficiently profitable, it may simply close down, or switch to providing services to another purchaser offering a better financial deal.

5. There is potential for great confusion if more than one public authority is contracting with the same provider for different services. Each will have their own standards and requirements which can lead to unhelpful competition, both in the fees to be paid and the shape of provision made.

From the provider perspective, there is a comparable list of disadvantages:

1. Voluntary organisations contracting for public services are in danger of losing their independence and compromising their basic values. The conditions of contracts, particularly those with criminal justice agencies, frequently involve the imposition of constraints on the user which runs contrary to the agency's philosophy of help voluntarily given and voluntarily received.

2. The administrative demands made by the tendering process and contract requirements, including a strong tendency to introduce performance related criteria, increases the time spent in paper work at the expense of direct service to the user.

3. Public service contracts leave the provider vulnerable to financial squeezing. The effect on an authority's cutback in expenditure is transferred immediately to the provider, who must handle closure of facilities and redundancies of staff. Failure to revalue grant can be even more problematic with providers expected to deliver the same level of services from a proportionately lower budget.

4. Competitive tendering can cause unhelpful divisions and mutual suspicion as agencies vie with each other for contracts by cutting costs and thereby quality.

Therefore, as probation committees and chief officers enter the era of cash limited budgets, anticipate the options which grant aiding provision will bring and consider the scope for partnership arrangements, what can be distilled from the experience of others?

The nature of the relationship between the probation service and voluntary organisations will almost certainly change and become more formal. Voluntary organisations are worried about loss of autonomy, the risk of becoming a subservient party in contract conditions dictated by the probation service, and being swamped with administrative paper work in return for modest, if not inadequate, funding. These fears need not be realised if probation services and voluntary organisations share discussion on the nature of the relationship they want with each other, and the following questions would merit consideration.

Firstly, should financial support be restricted to formal provision of service contracts, or is there value for both if an element of grant aid is provided to allow the voluntary organisation to pursue its other activities, such as campaigning and innovation?

Secondly, when contracts for a service are developed, what detail needs to be prescribed? Would it be better to keep such agreements as simple as possible, i.e. clarifying the expectation and responsibilities of both sides and not requiring over–complex monitoring which would detract from service provision? In other words, should the move be towards more formalised partnership agreements, rather than detailed business contracts?

Thirdly, is there any necessity for, or value in, competitive tendering? In most instances there are unlikely to be enough agencies 'in the business' to make this realistic and probation managers are likely to know with whom they wish to develop agreements. Competitive tendering is also likely to favour the larger national organisations at the expense of local community groups. If competitive tendering is not desirable, probation committees will need to give consideration to exempting offender service contracts from the provisions of Standing Orders.

Fourthly, what are the disadvantages in the probation service alone drawing up the terms of the contract/agreement and presenting it for acceptance? If the project does not run successfully, it could be claimed that the fault lay with the prescription writer. A jointly discussed and jointly developed contract is more likely to ensure a higher level of commitment to make it work.

Finally, how will pricing be determined? There are a number of potential approaches. The purchaser may offer a fee for the provision of services specified, and offer it to one or more voluntary organisations on a 'take it or leave it' basis. The resultant danger is that quantity may triumph over quality. An alternative is for the purchaser to ask the provider to cost the specification, which would then leave responsibility with the voluntary agency if it got things wrong. Whichever method is chosen, there would need to be some allowance for variation during the life of the contract, whether as the result of the purchaser wishing to change the nature or level of provision, or the provider needing to take account of pay or price increases.

What lessons have the managers and administrators in the US learned from their now quite extensive experience of purchase of service arrangements? One of the most comprehensive and useful assessments is that made by the Office of Purchased Services in Massachusetts which produced its final report in January 1990. This is a succinct review of twenty years' experience in a State where today purchase of service is virtually the only mode of delivering community based services. It is not without significance to the outcome that contracting was introduced as an expedient to overcome resistance to change by staff and unions, and the lack of State facilities in the community. In developing contracts the State applied its own policy procedures and systems without modification to the contract system. Purchasers treated providers as subdivisions of their own departments. Providers, mainly non–profit organisations with philanthropic origins, had inadequate business skills to negotiate effectively. The review of contract provision identified that what had developed from this background was:

- a massive contracting system which was encumbered with bureaucratic procedures and paper work

- providers servicing more and more users with inadequate financial resources

- a financially fragile and inefficient system, whose collapse could have devastating consequences for large sections of the community

The recommendations made to improve the system were based on three single principles:

- that the client comes first

- that consensus involving all parties to the contract should guide reform

- that both purchaser and provider must recognise the needs of the provider to survive as a business, in order to deliver effective services to clients.

The key elements of the redrafted contract regulations included:

1. A longer five year contract cycle (previously two to three years) to ensure greater stability, free resources from administration, and give time for evaluation of effectiveness.

2. A new format of contract which gave power to meeting client need.

3. A recognition that the provider agency is a business enterprise, and must acquire resources in the real world at real world prices including, importantly, a recognition that workers in the provider agency had to be paid salaries sufficient to ensure good quality appointments and reduce staff turnover.

4. The replacement of line item contract budgets with a single price agreement, giving providers flexibility in managing budgets.

An important additional response was to create an Institute for Community Services to bring together individual providers, academics, clients and their advocates, funders, the business sector, politicians, and administrators, to address issues of human service policy and practice. Among the aims of the Institute are the development of standards for professional conduct and practice accreditation, the coordination of research, the development of programme performance objectives, the creation of long term policy, and to advocate for change.

Whilst emphasis is also given to developing performance based contracting, this is seen as a separate venture and caution is urged in not creating new complex and burdensome bureaucratic procedures, which only again divert resources and focus from service delivery to clients.

References

Audit Commission (1991) Going straight: Developing Good Practice in the Probation Service, Occasional Paper No 16.

13 Probation management structures and partnerships in America: lessons for England

Lucia Saiger

Introduction

In 1991 I was awarded a travelling fellowship from the Winston Churchill Trust. The purpose of this award was to visit the USA to study the different approaches to drug and alcohol dependent offenders. The observations made in this chapter are based on time spent with the Federal Probation Department in New York City and Buffalo, and the New York City department of probation. I also visited the director of probation in Washington DC. Due to the practice of contracting out services for drug and alcohol offenders I also spent some time with a variety of service providers.

I arrived in New York having been appointed middle manager in the Cleveland probation service only six months before the trip. The Cleveland service works to a well–defined set of objectives and targets and, as a newly appointed middle manager, I was interested in probation management structures in the USA and how these linked to the provision of drug treatment for offenders. Consequently my aim in this chapter is to focus on the structure used by probation services in the USA to manage and evaluate services for offenders which have been contracted out. It is not my intention to describe in any detail the drug treatment provided.

Drugs and crime

To understand the emphasis placed on providing drug treatment and the organisation of staff to work with drug offenders by both the Federal and New York City probation department, it is useful to acknowledge the link between drugs and crime which has been made in numerous American publications (Court Accounting Office, 1988). State and local policy makers and criminal justice practitioners are having to respond to this problem by the development of effective policies. In the process of doing this economic considerations are important and during my time in New York I often heard the argument of cost to favour treatment before incarceration. Although it was accepted that treatment is more effective in reducing drug use and crime, when arguing for more resources and in trying to convince the public, what was emphasised was that it was cheaper to do this in the community rather than in custodial institutions. In a system where money is allocated specifically to obtain services for drug treatment and where the use of this money is monitored and evaluated in terms of how many individuals are treated, it is inevitable that the principle of value for money was a priority.

Federal probation department

Both in the New York City and Buffalo departments there was a probation officer responsible for contracts with service providers for drug treatment. Within this role the probation officer performed two functions. First, he was responsible for providing 'Purchase Order Clauses–Terms of Agreement' to not–for–profit service providers. Following the bids from service providers he evaluated what was on offer and made decisions based crudely on the following criteria: 50% quality, 25% price, 15% business reputation and 10% location. The structure for service providers to adhere to is rigid and lengthy and includes access by the court and authorised representatives to inspect, monitor and evaluate the work of the contractor. It provides clear guidelines concerning the information to be provided to the probation service which basically includes client records, availability to staff to discuss the treatment of a client, programme plans, outcomes, results of urine tests etc. It is interesting that the probation service, within the context of the contract established with the treatment provider, maintained as much control as possible through strict guidelines.

The treatment provider would also be visited every three months by the probation officer who would check financial systems, client records and client signing-in logs, against bills paid. If the probation service was dissatisfied with the service being provided they would, after giving clear objectives for improvement over a given period of time, opt out of the contract if improvements had not occurred.

The overall review of contracts between the probation service and not–for–profit organisations resides with a central office in Washington DC. I visited this department and found their knowledge of contracted out service provision within each federal probation service throughout the US incredibly extensive. This department cedes control to areas to arrange their own services but they have an evaluation and monitoring system to ensure that money is being spent appropriately within each federal agency.

The second function performed by the probation officer was to coordinate referrals to the service providers. Within the probation department he held information on access to services provided in the community, paid for by the probation service. Probation officers dealing specifically with drug offenders would go through a central referral point to obtain services for the client. In this way equality of opportunity is afforded to every offender in terms of the treatment available. Monitoring that drug offenders proceed through the central referral system is undertaken by the supervising probation officer when scrutinising the caseloads of probation officers.

New York city probation department

A drugs coordinator was employed by the New York City probation department to undertake the role performed within the federal system. However, the individual employed in New York was not a probation officer. A recent grant had enabled the probation department to fund 12,000 treatment places for drug offenders and the drug coordinator had established ten contracts with not–for–profit agencies to provide services for offenders. Again the criteria for monitoring and evaluation are strict and services provided are checked regularly by the drugs coordinator. Furthermore, the federal system is duplicated in the sense that probation officers have access through a central referral point for treatment services available for their client. In addition, specialised teams such as Intensive Supervision Programmes (ISP) and Substance Abuse Verification Enforcement (SAVE) deal specifically with offenders with drug problems.

Obtaining services from outside agencies is seen very much as developing resources which enable probation officers to do their job more efficiently and effectively which includes protecting the public and the rehabilitation of offenders. Law enforcement and probationers adhering to the requirement within statutory court orders are seen as effective probation work, but these go hand–in–hand with the principle of care. The element of compulsion within a statutory requirement was not seen as detrimental to an offender but as a mechanism through which the offender would be encouraged to do something about his or her life. Using treatment services provided by agencies outside the probation service is the norm which does not detract from the probation officer's case management. In fact, in my opinion, this arrangement serves to clarify the role expectation of the probation officer and the requirements the probationer must fulfil in terms of behaviour, whereabouts and responsibilities. For as the drugs coordinator stated 'control and relationship are not in opposition. If you do not put some order back into a disordered life how can any treatment begin to be effective'. Probation officers have a concern for individual offenders and as such they want the treatment provided by other agencies to be effective, but this does not detract from their role as law enforcement officers and working towards the probationer living within a framework of conditions set by the court.

The middle manager role

Having had six months experience working as a middle manager prior to visiting America, I was interested in how this role functioned in the United States. In my meetings with middle managers in both federal and city probation departments it was evident that they viewed their role in terms of monitoring service delivery. Probation practice in the New York department of probation was directed through an 'Adult Services Supervision Manual and Guidelines'. This manual explained the primary responsibility of the probation service which was to supervise adult probationers, taking account of the need to provide public protection and preparing probationers for an independent and law abiding life. The manual gives explicit step–by–step directions on how the probation officer should perform his or her functions when supervising offenders. Offenders undertake a computerised risk assessment which is accomplished by completing a risk assessment instrument which evaluates an offender's probable risk of failure during the supervision period. The offender is then assigned to one of four levels of risk – high, medium, low or minimal – based upon risk assessment which takes cognizance of social, legal and demographic information.

Subsequently this information is attached to the case record and is available for the middle manager. Risk levels cannot change unless the middle manager agrees. The number of contacts with different levels of offender is clearly stated as well as the contacts probation officers are required to make with treatment providers. All information is recorded on case files on standardised forms which makes it relatively easy for the middle manager to check information and to be satisfied that all necessary tasks are being undertaken. If there is any deviation from the guidelines this must be justified and explained to the middle manager. The probation officer expects the line manager to monitor performance in relation to specific guidelines with the result that they did not become debilitated by arguments concerning probation officer autonomy, which sometimes bedevils probation work in England.

Probation officers in the USA systematically checked with offenders that they were complying with probation order conditions. This required written evidence of such things as employment, attendance at drug treatment facilities, reporting for urine testing, fine repayments and correct address. Every time an offender reported to the probation officer they would sign the case record as proof of attendance. Although this may appear excessively controlling, compared to the situation in England, in my opinion it is a system which leaves little room for ambiguity in terms of the role of the probation officer in supervising the offender, the expectations on the offender to fulfil the requirements of court orders, and what the middle manager has to do to ensure that public money is being spent appropriately and that probation officers are doing their job.

The system of management in the federal system was much the same in that case records had standardised forms with offenders classified according to risk. One aspect more clearly evident within the federal system was the degree of computerisation. Each middle manager would computerise information on officer caseloads including programme plans for offenders and dates for target achievement. If these were not achieved it would be recorded on the computer and would form part of the officer's evaluation. Along with monitoring caseloads, presentence investigation reports were read by middle managers prior to court appearance and subsequent performance information would be computerised. This information would include errors made in the report, date submitted to court, recommendation and outcome. Again the middle manager would review all this information on the computer at the appropriate time to scrutinise performance which would form part of the officer's evaluation.

One interesting facet in the federal system was that should a probation officer not perform according to expectations, the officer would not receive an annual financial increment and would be provided with a planned programme of work to ensure improvement. If this did not yield desired results then the officer would cease to be employed. By contrast, should a probation officer show exceptional performance standards and commitment then she/he would receive a 'quality step' increase as well as the annual increment. It is possible that what I saw in the US is a precursor for developments within the English probation system. Notwithstanding objections, I believe there could be a place for such a system of evaluating an officer's performance against objectives and targets which would result in suitable remuneration if targets have been reached which will include the successful completion of court orders, reductions in problem areas, and a reduction in criminal activity. There is certainly much food for thought in the way the American system of probation operates.

It was clear to me from my discussions with middle managers in America that their role was clear because the probation officer role was clear. Furthermore the expectations probation staff had of offenders was clear in the sense that they were expected to comply with court orders. Within this process social work treatment was undertaken by other agencies within the community, which allowed the probation officer to exercise a law enforcement role with offenders. Perhaps if the English probation service moved towards a similar structure, greater numbers of offenders could be managed in the community and afforded the opportunity of social work help by other agencies. Obviously a change in direction of probation officer role would be required if partnerships were to be developed with a variety of service providers. I certainly feel that explicit directions from central government on the future probation task and how to incorporate the voluntary sector in the process of managing offenders in the community is essential. Consequently, middle managers would have a more clear view of their own role. Although probation staff in the USA were overworked because caseloads were high, being certain that social work treatment is carried out in the community by those with expertise in specific problem areas, meant that offender problems were addressed. In the English system, of course, it is the task of the probation officer to provide all the elements of supervision i.e. social work help, treatment, and control. From my point of view this does not guarantee that the probation officer will provide all these elements or that the officer has the capacity and skill to address all those problems which may be presented by the offender. Therefore, a review of the role of the probation officer in England is required, particularly as we move towards having to come to terms with the implications of the 1991 Criminal Justice Act.

Employee assistance programme

Another interesting facet of managing staff within the New York city department of probation emerged in February 1987 with the creation of the employee assistance programme. After monitoring staff absenteeism it was decided to offer staff a service to deal with problems affecting job performance. In conversation with the worker who organised provision in New York she described the service as a way of helping employees with personal problems before they became personnel problems. The service provided is strictly confidential, voluntary and detached from the discipline system. On average the worker counselled 5 to 7 individuals per week. The investment for the middle manager in referring staff to this programme is that personal problems can be dealt with outside the supervision process which hopefully produces a rapid response by the worker to deal with problems and thus enhance work performance. If the problem is too serious that a further referral is required, this would be highlighted by the programme worker who would liaise with personnel to organise such things as leave for the probation officer. The middle manager could then organise staff to take account of the absence of a member of staff. Also in the longer term if staff have been given the opportunity of help through the employee assistance programme but problems continued to affect performance, they could not deny that help had been offered to resolve problem areas. The evidence suggests that this system had reduced staff absenteeism and alleviated levels of stress within the workforce. Moreover the cost of providing such a service seemed to pay for itself because it resulted in fewer days lost to illness and performance levels improved.

Conclusion

My experience in New York was exciting and very illuminating. Although I was staggered by the number of offenders supervised by probation officers (on average some 150 offenders per officer), when I understood the different roles performed by officers in the

USA compared with England, it began to make sense how so many could be supervised. What did surprise me was that even though probation officers were not primarily employed as social workers, nevertheless the level of care demonstrated towards their client group was similar to that which we like to think underpins the service in England.

Probation officers in the USA had a strong value system which was to help offenders to be reintegrated into society and also to stop them from abusing themselves. In this process they had few difficulties with the concept of control which has created problems for probation staff in England. Furthermore, confrontation, challenge and honesty accompanied interview techniques. In a society where drug use is a vicious phenomenon and where offenders have experienced difficult lives, probation officers need to be tough. Middle managers in a world of competing resources and costs ensured that government money was spent correctly, both within the service and where money was spent on service providers. The use of technology and the rapid flow of data were essential tools in caseload management.

Having returned from America towards the end of 1991 I feel that the probation service in England needs to be honest with itself about its future role within the criminal justice system. Training, value systems in a changing culture, partnerships with the voluntary sector, workloads, measures of effectiveness, employment conditions, and developments associated with technology, are just some of the issues which need to be addressed during the 1990s. In this process perhaps probation management structures in the United States have something to contribute to our thinking.

References

Court Accounting Office (1988) Controlling Drug Abuse: A Status Report.

14 Conclusion: an agenda for the future

Roger Statham and Philip Whitehead

The pace of change often referred to in this book has been taxing for probation service staff for over a decade and the coping abilities of the organisation have been tested to the full. Change has been so rapid and frequent that there has been little or no time to assimilate or consolidate before another dose of change has been inflicted. These events are having an enormous impact as the contributors to this book have readily testified. There are also acute tensions within the service and the discomfort is likely to proceed unabated for the foreseeable future. Furthermore, the implied threat that other alternatives may be sought should the service fail to deliver following the implementation of the 1991 Criminal Justice Act will not, unfortunately, go away.

This book has provided the opportunity to highlight a number of issues facing the service and against this background we think it would be useful in the concluding chapter to speculate about further changes that might flow from the fluidity of the present situation. The risk of being wrong does not invalidate this exercise in sticking out our editorial necks and waiting for the axe to fall, because it is designed to stimulate the imaginations of those readers with greater perspicacity than the editors themselves. It has to be said that the perspective which follows will be developed from a particular managerial viewpoint; not simply to reinforce the theme of the book but to emphasise the importance of leadership at a time when organisation is destabilised. We use the word destabilised because even though change has affected the culture of the service, it is still too early to discern recognisable future patterns, even though there are one or two signposts showing the shape of things to come.

Cash limits and related issues

Cash limits have concentrated the mind wonderfully on filthy lucre during 1991/92. Whilst some areas have emerged from the application of the formula in a better position than others, it is our view that cash limits will have a profound effect on the consciousness of the service. The cry 'can we afford it?' will be heard increasingly if there are insufficient resources to run service operations. This factor, coupled with grant aiding powers, may push probation committees to think about cheaper options for service provision. The service is becoming familiar with the concept of purchaser/provider, but what does this really mean and what could be the implications? Might the purchaser route be taken solely because of economic factors and, if so, where does this leave notions of quality assurance? Any organisation providing services to customers-customers has to consider the economics of service provision. Are there cheaper alternatives available? A local probation service faced with a budget shortfall may be more inclined to answer this question by initiating a detailed examination of the tasks undertaken and the competences required. A logical next step would be to ensure that work performed by probation officers which does not require 'professional social work skills' may well have to be diverted to other members of staff. This departure in itself may lead to a realignment of the workforce in terms of those in possession of social work qualifications and others not so trained. This kind of thinking is also reflected in the likelihood of other organisations providing services on behalf of, or in conjunction with, local probation services. The partnership debate illustrated above by the experiences of the USA and Northern Ireland, and the reality of probation committees acquiring grant aiding powers, makes this development inevitable.

The economic reality of this scenario is put into sharper focus by the potential extra cost of probation officers as a consequence of the unsocial hours agreement, because the extra money needed to pay for this agreement must be found within the constraints of a cash limited budget. There is not any extra money to pay for this demand because the Home Office will no longer provide a blank cheque safety net for area services; rather the agreement will have to be funded by taking money from other areas of activity which could mean, for example, less money for new developments or training. There can be no doubt that the demands of cash limits will, in time, radically affect the behaviour of the organisation and it can only be hoped, in the short term, that there is sufficient cash to meet the demands of the new Criminal Justice Act from October 1992, in addition to existing demands.

The development of core cluster arrangements associated with approved hostels has provided a timely example of staff being recruited for a specific role, working unsocial hours, and requiring no little skill. We are not aware that probation officers had been considered for this role. Whilst the costs of employing probation officers has continued to grow, service managers have been recruiting a new group within the workforce who are providing flexibility and economy. It follows that the quality of probation practice, notions of excellence and economy, efficiency and effectiveness of service delivery will become important issues for all staff within the service during the 1990s, but particularly for probation officers. This is because they will be the most expensive staff group and only through the effectiveness of their performance will this provision be secured and resourced.

At first sight this may appear to be an extreme view of likely future events; but coming up on the blind side are potential partners who could take on board tasks previously undertaken by probation officers. Local probation areas who are stretched to make ends meet will undoubtedly begin to think about these and other options, particularly when suggested by treasurers and finance managers who are not captured by service history, culture and tradition. As a consequence, hostels, programmes for certain types of offenders which include those on community supervision and post–custody supervision, aspects of community service, might well come to be delivered through the purchaser option. However unpalatable some of this might impact on one's traditional understanding of the probation service, it does seem as though some aspects have an air of inevitability about them and for some the threat of privatisation remains.

Equal opportunities

Another interesting potential development is related to the notion of equality of opportunity and the growth of consumerism. The idea of offenders as consumers of services and making demands about standards may seem a little extraordinary. On the other hand it might simply be seen as an extension of contract work with individuals under supervision. One is tempted to ask: just how user friendly is the probation service to its clients? Are disaffected offenders convinced that probation officers are going out of their way to provide the best service possible? What rights do offenders have and what standards of care can they expect? In future it will be important to balance the demands of a criminal justice system which expects offenders to exercise responsibility towards other people in their local communities, with their right to citizenship and access to political, social and economic opportunities like the rest of us.

Corporate performance

Furthermore, one may pose the question of whether, at this particular stage in the history of the service, probation officers are more preoccupied with their own professional issues than those of the groups they are supposed to be 'advising, assisting and befriending'? Returning to Mintzberg's notion of the professional bureaucracy which was touched upon in chapter 4, this type of organisational structure may not only result in some professionals ignoring the needs of clients; it may also encourage them to ignore the needs of the organisation. However, as Mintzberg reminds us 'the organisation has need for loyalty too – to support its own strategies, to staff its administrative committees, to see it through conflicts with the professional association' (Mintzberg, 1983, p208–209). Notwithstanding the arguments which could emanate from pursuing some of Mintzberg's ideas, the survival of the service in the 1990s will depend on probation officers being committed to an organisation which delivers a quality service to consumers and which satisfies customers and stakeholders. Concomitantly, the notion of each individual member of the organisation uniquely contributing to corporate excellence, under-pinned by national standards, will become important.

The nature of the organisation is also an issue. Is it a 'bottom-up' organisation, which has been suggested in the past, or do contemporary circumstances challenge this assumption? We are left thinking that the demands created by national standards and cash limits necessitate clear and well organised management and leadership. This, in turn, will increase accountability within the service that is unlikely to fade with the passing of time. The idea that practice can be left solely in the hands of a group of com-mitted and self–actualised individuals no longer has a ring of credibility following the insights into areas of practice provided by both internal and Home Office inspections. Moreover, the recently published report by the Association of Chief Officers of Probation ACOP (1982) which looks at offenders as the victims of crime, yields some salutary insights. Through the eyes of these victims we can see the shortcomings of those institutions designed to bring care and control to society. The report not only reflects the difficulties probation officers have in reaching some of these people but equally illustrates the way practice has drifted.

One other dimension of corporate performance requires consideration which is the metamorphosis of probation committees into probation boards. Breidge Gadd in chapter 11 examined some of the issues from a Northern Ireland perspective. Whilst the proposed arrangements for England and Wales differ in some respects, the intentions are similar (Home Office, 1992). The advent of probation boards are designed to bolster the role of committees and there is a clear commitment to involve the board in policy and strategy. Interestingly, the chief probation officer is to be a member of the board in the role of chief executive. Although there will be a period for consultation the changes are likely to facilitate accountability in the service.

Opportunities in local communities

Whilst there will be many challenges to respond to during the next few years, we should also acknowledge that there are opportunities to be grasped. Should the philosophy and potential of the 1991 Criminal Justice Act be realised, the probation service could be playing a much more important role in managing and maintaining high risk offenders within local communities. If we can achieve a reduction in the number of offenders going into Young Offender Institutions and Prisons through the greater use of community sentences, this would be a major achievement. Unfortunately history is not on our side; but there is an opportunity to create it. To achieve this result all agencies who comprise the criminal justice system will have to cooperate in ways they haven't in the past, and the community will have to be reassured that the criminal justice system is able to manage, contain and control more serious offenders in the community. This means dealing imaginatively with the issues of fear of crime and risk which opens up the possibility of a key role for the probation service. Drawing upon its traditional values of care, understanding, tolerance, sympathy and notions of citizenship for all members of a community, it could still become a key player in facilitating shared working with criminal justice partners and others to achieve the reintegration of the disaffected and vulnerable into local communities.

Furthermore, it is important to remember at a time when the demands of economy, efficiency and value for money are in the

ascendant, that there must remain a moral and humane dimension to criminal justice work to which the probation service can
still make a unique contribution. What we mean by this was well
illustrated by William Temple in the 1930s when he said that

> We are not what we appear, but what we are becoming, and if
> that is what we truly are, no penal system is fully just which
> treats us as anything else. For this reason also it is true that
> though retribution is the most fundamental element in penal
> action, and deterrence for practical reasons the most
> indispensable, yet the reformative element is not only the most
> valuable in the sympathy which it exhibits and in the effects
> which it produces, but is also that which alone confers upon
> the other two the full quality of justice. It is here that the
> whole system of Probation fits into the scheme; ... the work of
> Probation Officers ... should not be regarded as a dispensable
> though estimable adjunct to the administration of justice, but
> as an essential part of it without which it cannot be altogether
> just (Temple, 1934, p39–40).

Moving on, the possibility of the probation and prison services
being part of a joint Home Office department, or even a ministry
of justice, are possible developments in the future. As governors
begin to recognise the value of community links and the prison
building programme opens up greater potential for truly local
prisons, there could be a move towards even greater voluntary
sector involvement with the prison operation. This could result in
a much greater ownership of offenders by local communities and
improved support networks within these communities.

Therefore, whilst there are a number of issues around at the
present time which indubitably provoke anxiety, we should not be
overly negative because there are also opportunities to take
advantage of. However, to take advantage of these opportunities it
will be important for the probation service to move on quickly
from being client–casework centred to become a more diversified
organisation. The rationale for this has recently been well argued
by Robert Harris (1992) who says that, during the 1990s, the
probation service will have to work with other criminal justice
agencies in the spheres of public relations, crime prevention,
combating the fear of crime, risk reduction and victim support
work, to name but a few. But given the adept academic that he is,
he focuses primarily on the 'what' and 'why' issues i.e. this is
'what' the probation service should be doing and this is 'why' it
should be doing it. However, the challenge for the service is to
translate the 'what' and 'why' into the 'how'. In fact, Harris's
book neatly clarifies the differences between the interested

academic onlooker on the probation scene on the one hand, and the probation manager who has to deal with the 'how' and strategic dimension. How should the probation service undertake crime prevention work? How should the service work with the victims of crime? How should the service develop partnerships? These are complex yet critical questions which have to be answered by managers during the 1990s.

ACOP – taking the initiative

But who will take on these management issues? In other words, which service organisation should be at the forefront of such developments? It may be argued that the National Association of Probation Officers (NAPO) has, to some extent, set its face against aspects of the management process; and the National Association of Senior Probation Officers (NASPO) has still to emerge as a major player. The Central Council of Probation Committees (CCPC) is likely to be largely preoccupied with its own changing world as probation boards emerge in the near future. This leaves ACPO as the major (perhaps only) vehicle for developing management thinking in the probation service. At this stage, however, the way in which it will do this is a matter of speculation. Consequently, we will have to content ourselves by saying that ACOP should be more overtly management orientated and provide management leadership. The difficulties of speaking for the fifty-five area services when there is no consensus concerning what is meant by management, should be acknowledged; but the need for a clear management lead has never been more apparent. The shaping of management ideas, principles and strategies is essential if the service is to adapt itself to the agenda of the 1990s. But what are the elements of this agenda? An attempt to sketch an answer to this question is provided in the final section.

An agenda for the 1990s

Firstly, it is imperative to clarify the nature and rationale of the organisation which includes a clear statement of priorities, policies, objectives and targets. Once this has been done it is equally imperative to determine the organisational structure (or configuration to use one of the Mintzberg's terms) required to implement policies, achieve objectives and reach targets. This means that the service must understand the implications of probation boards, look again at the roles of senior managers,

middle managers and main grade probation officers, in addition
to the roles of information, finance and personnel managers,
secretaries, administrative, clerical and ancillary staff. Consequently, organisational rationale and structure should be
re–evaluated at all levels.

Secondly, the service must become a results oriented organisation. All spheres of activity must be purposeful, with specific
expectations of what is intended to be achieved. The service has
become a key player in the criminal justice system and in order to
capitalise on this, careful thought must be given to critical success
factors. In clarifying these, particular attention needs to be given
to defining the measures of success to be employed, which is
easier said than done.

Thirdly, in order to deliver results we must develop a strategic
thinking and planning approach in all areas of work on a
continuum which will begin with work allocation through to the
results of individual performance measured by making best use of
information. Furthermore we need strategies for working with
other criminal justice agencies, managing risk and fear of crime,
managing more serious offenders in the community, victim
support work, partnerships, gender and race issues. The task is to
translate the 'what' and 'why' questions associated with different
areas of work into clarifying 'how' the work should be undertaken
and achieved. This will require implementation strategies of
clarity and precision and as such will add a degree of sophistication to management processes. This is perhaps the most
important area in which rigorous thinking will have to be done
during the next few years.

Fourthly, the social policy dimension must remain a central
component of probation work, despite attempts by the New Right
during the 1980s to divert attention away from the social
conditions and the social structure towards blaming individuals
for crime. Probation officers are well aware of a high proportion
of offenders who are poor, have no educational qualifications, are
unemployed, with numerous problems which are related to their
socio–economic status, and don't have a stake within society.
Many offenders are relatively poor which, as Davidson and
Erskine (1992) remind us, results in various forms of exclusion of
an economic, social and political nature. These are important
issues for the probation service to engage with which have implications for the future of citizenship and social justice (and are
themes discussed in more detail by Whitehead, 1992).

Fifthly, the implications of this agenda for probation officer
training should be re–evaluated. If the probation service is about
to develop a more management oriented culture during the next

decade, this has implications for the curriculum of those trainers in universities and polytechnics who prepare probation students to enter the organisation. Probation officers of the future must have an understanding of the politics of crime and the expectations of government, of organisational policies, objectives, targets dynamics, management process and strategic thinking; be part of a corporate culture which demands high standards of performance; understand the importance of producing accurate information on offenders which contributes to determining an area's cash limit allocation; an understanding of national standards and practice guidelines which are the arbiters of good practice. In other words there must be a closer fit between the type of probation officer required in the organisation and the curriculum of training establishments. These changes must also provide the opportunity to look at the individual effectiveness of those seeking to be part of the workforce.

However, this five point agenda will require existing staff within the organisation to adapt to a changing situation, and to help us to come to terms with this we turn to some useful ideas expressed by Charles Handy. Handy is acutely aware that the working environment is rapidly changing and that this has implications for organisations. In such a world he gives the following advice:

> Looking at things upside down, or back to front, or inside
> out, is a way of stimulating the imagination, of spurring our
> creativity in an Age of Unreason when things are not going to
> go on working as they have been working, whether we like it
> or not ... A changing world needs new ideas (1990,
> p.200–201).

Applying these thoughts to the probation service we can say that what we have tried to do in this book is stimulate the reader's imagination concerning the future of the organisation and the place of management within it. To take on board some of the ideas in this book will require people to change, and to keep on changing, which is an uncomfortable process. But, as Handy reminds us, 'Change, after all, is only another word for growth, another synonym for learning. We can all do it, and enjoy it, if we want to' (1990, p.4).

Our response to Handy's challenge is to suggest that the probation service's preparedness to change will probably determine its future during the 1990s and beyond. We can, however, offer the reader a few words of reassurance; the language between Leeson (1914) and Statham (1990) has changed, but the values have not.

References

ACOP (1992) 'A sense of justice: offenders As victims of crime'. A research report by M. Peelo, J. Stewart, G. Stewart and A. Prior, University of Lancaster.

Davidson, R. and Erskine, A. (eds) (1992) *Poverty, Deprivation and Social Work*, Jessica Kingsley.

Handy, C. (1990) *The Age of Unreason*, Arrow Books

Harris, R. (1992) *Crime, Criminal Justice and the Probation Service*, Tavistock/Routledge.

Home Office (1992) *Organising Supervision and Punishment in the Community: Consultation on Probation Committee Reforms and of Liaison with Sentencers*, CPO 19/1992, HMSO.

Leeson, C. (1914) *The Probation System*, P and S King and Son.

Mintzberg, H. (1983) *Structure in Fives: Designing Effective Organisations*, Prentice Hall International.

Statham, R. S. (1990) *Probation in the Market Driven World*, Cleveland Probation Service.

Temple, W. (1934) *The Ethics Of Penal Action*, The Clarke Hall Fellowship.

Whitehead, P. (1992) 'The probation service and the church: A theoretical rationale For partnership', *Crucible*.